SECRET LIFE OF A JUROR:

VOIR DIRE

The Domestic Violence Query

By

Paul Sanders

Book formatting and cover design:
www.bookclaw.com

Author photo credit @ Investigation Discovery/Deadly Sins

CreateSpace Independent Publishing Platform North Charleston, SC

Library of Congress Control Number: 2018910839

First Edition March 2018
Second Edition October 2018

Available as eBook, Paperback and Audio Book

Awards:

- *2018 Best Book Awards - Finalist "Law" - Copyright 15th Annual Awards Sponsored by American Book Fest*

- *2018 Readers' Favorite Five Stars – Copyright Readers' Favorite Book Reviews and Award Contest*

- *2018 Best Book Awards – Finalist "Young Adult: Non-Fiction" – Copyright 15th Annual Awards Sponsored by American Book Fest.*

Dedicated to my brother and to all victims of domestic violence.

We are survivors.

With special acknowledgements to:

- ❖ *KC Wuraftic*
- ❖ *Mary-Margaret Spallone*
- ❖ *Gloria Norris*
- ❖ *Mr. and Mrs. Clifton Fadiman*
- ❖ *Susan Sandler*
- ❖ *Steve Ross*
- ❖ *Michael Korda*
- ❖ *Arnold Dolin*
- ❖ *Leslie Schnur*
- ❖ *Neil Nyren*
- ❖ *Kevin Elde- Seattle Computers*
- ❖ *Taylor Castillo*
- ❖ *Donna Gilligan-Miller*
- ❖ *Tiffany St. Claire*
- ❖ *Sue Meierotto*
- ❖ *Emily Wasko*

"...Once in a while
you get shown the Light
in the strangest of places
if you look at it right."

Robert Hunter
Scarlet Begonias

CONTENTS

Voir Dire

(Vwah-Dear)

Noun: the act or process of questioning prospective jurors to determine which are qualified (as by freedom from bias) and suited for service on a jury.

(Merriam Webster)

CHAPTER 1

THE FIRST DAY

My story began with a simple prayer, one that I had said one thousand four hundred and sixty days in a row. It was my fourth AA birthday and I felt I had graduated into a new life. My first two years of sobriety had been spent learning how not to take a drink one day at a time. In my third year, my junior year of sobriety, I forgave God, myself and those who had wronged me and those I had wronged. Once I reached my fourth year, I thought I had reached a comfort zone where alcohol was no longer a part of my life.

"God grant me the serenity to accept the things I cannot change, the courage to change the things I can and the wisdom to know the difference," I said as fervently as I had every day. "I am grateful for everything God has given me; such as the roof over my head, food in my stomach and the strength to remain sober each day. I am grateful for both my bartending job and my EBay business selling Hot Wheels. If this is what You want me to do in life, then I am content. If there is something more, I am ready."

Twenty days later, I responded to a simple jury summons.

There are some who would say that my being a death penalty juror went on to change my life. I am honored and grateful for the experience. It was not the trial that caused such a change but a simple question on voir dire, the first phase a juror must go through in the selection process.

The French translation of voir dire means 'to see, to say'. For the thousands that respond to their jury summons, it is simply a questioning process. In a murder trial, voir dire will have a written and a verbal phase and can be expected to be intricate and detailed. Every questionnaire given to potential jurors is customized to each particular trial. Each juror is given the same questionnaire.

"Take whatever amount of time you need to answer each question carefully and thoughtfully. You may not speak to anyone while completing your questionnaire. Should there be any questions which you would like kept private from the open courtroom, please note as such. We will arrange a meeting with all the attorneys and judge outside the presence of the other jurors," a bailiff directed. She adjusted the glasses on her nose. "Remember, your honesty is critical and the court thanks you. You may now begin your questionnaire."

If one did not know any better, the group of people tackling their questionnaire could just as well have been students completing a college prep exam. The court assistants watched everyone as the rustle of paper filled the air, each potential juror aggressively handling their task.

I flipped through the quarter inch thick packet. There were over one hundred questions each formatted similarly: question, an affirmative or negative response and a 'please explain' section followed by five blank lines to complete a response.

The questionnaire began innocuously enough with basic statistical questions which I dutifully answered. I had been born in 1961 in Texas and spent my formative years in Michigan. My father was an oral surgeon and my mother, although trained as a nurse, stayed at home to raise the family. My paternal grandfather had been a foreman for General Motors in Detroit while my maternal grandfather had been vice president of Cadillac for the better part of forty years. I responded that I had a brother named Mark and a sister named Louise, the fraternal twin to Mark.

When asked how my relationship was with my immediate family, I penned in, 'estranged'.

I took a moment and looked around at the others busily doing their work. Many were guarding their work from the on-looking eyes of others around them. I stretched my fingers and dove back in. I could not help thinking that the questions were an easier task than I had expected.

My strategy in completing the series of questions was simple. I would be honest and when the response required an explanation, I kept the sentences limited and avoided being too wordy. I assumed they were looking for truth to the best of my ability but it did not require a novel written in response. When in doubt, I would be as honest and forthright as I could.

The next series of questions listed a series of names and asked whether I knew any of the names and in what context. I guessed that these were participants in the trial including the defendant, her attorneys and names of the prosecutors. I did not know any of them and checked the 'no' box next to each name.

When asked about any prior juror experiences, I stated that I had never been a juror on a trial even though I had responded to multiple jury notices in a variety of states. When asked whether I wanted to be a juror for this trial, I answered affirmatively. I explained that it would be an honor to perform jury duty and it would be a great way to contribute back to society. I felt I would be a good juror.

The first time I saw the question asking whether I had ever experienced domestic violence in my household, whether directly or by observation, I quickly checked the 'no' box and moved on. I lived alone and did not like mean people.

It was not until I reached an inquiry about whether I had ever been incarcerated longer than thirty days, including my juvenile years, did I stop and pause. I ran my fingers through my hair and looked from my paperwork. I was suddenly uncomfortable. I wondered if there would be a record of it somewhere.

I had been incarcerated longer than thirty days in 1976. I pondered whether I should avoid mention of it. I had not expected the question and I had managed to keep all of it tucked away in a little box in my mind. It made me realize that I had answered the domestic violence question incorrectly.

I wanted to be on the jury but would my incarceration of many years ago work against me? What of my experience with domestic violence? Should I leave it all wrapped up in that tiny box in my far distant memory or should I reveal a truth I no longer wanted to think about? Could I get away with making no mention of it or should I risk it all by stating what happened?

The memories were dark, dirty and tainted with pain and discomfort. I spent my whole life forgetting about it and there it was in front of me. How could I explain in two short sentences what happened without my looking like a criminal once again?

I squirmed in my chair and flipped the pages back on the voir dire to the question which referenced domestic violence. Although I had denied experiencing domestic violence, I had not thought of it in the context of my childhood. It was natural that I first thought of domestic violence as spousal abuse. Most people think of it in those terms I knew at that moment that my greatest test of honesty was the response to that particular question.

I slowly checked the box 'yes' although I did not change my negative answer. I looked at the blank lines which begged my answer under 'please explain'. How could I explain in such few words the terrors that dominated my life beginning in 1970?

My pen was frozen in my fingers, the ballpoint touched the paper. I struggled to find the words. I did not know then that this would be my most important response.

There was a picture that sat in my father's study for many years. It was taken on Easter Sunday during a flawless, sunny day in Marquette, Michigan. A family of five stood in front of a big beautiful house. On the left was Louise, just seven years-old. Her long black hair, held in place by barrettes, rested softly on her shoulders. She was smiling with her hands at her sides while wearing a white jacket over a knee-length green dress.

Momma stood next to her. She resembled Jacqueline Kennedy with her perfectly sculpted dark hair and photogenic smile. She wore a blue knit dress accented by a light blue jacket and high heels. Everything looked right in the world.

Her height was dwarfed somewhat by Daddy's six-foot-two height. He wore a navy blue suit, white shirt and striped blue tie. As always, he wore black wing-tipped shoes. His smile toward the camera was warm and inviting. He held Momma's hand.

Mark, also just seven years old, stood next to Daddy. He looked a little out of sorts in his black suit but smiled just the same.

I stood next to my brother, three years seniority was reflected in my marked height difference. I wore glasses, a blue suit and black patent leather shoes which reflected the sunlight. I smiled toward the camera, not because I was happy but because I was supposed to.

The house stood behind our family. It was a three-story English Tudor-styled home set atop a two hundred foot heated driveway at the end of a cul-de-sac. The lawn and bushes and trees were perfectly manicured. It made the home look grander and larger. It was arguably one of the most beautiful homes in all of northern Michigan.

In a split second, as my pen lay prone, I thought of that picture and everything behind it. They say that one's life flashes before one's eyes in the final moments before death which would have been similar to what happened to me. I struggled to find the words because the picture in my mind of the 'happy' family presented, was not what happened behind closed doors.

This family had a terrible secret hidden behind their smiles.

I remembered what it was like to be ten-years-old as if I were watching it through a camera lens. It was a memory that I seemed to watch from afar, from a different place. It was memory I had kept sealed and locked in my mind because nobody had ever asked about it

For every potential juror who has experienced domestic violence and had to answer the question in voir dire, each has a different story about being a victim.

This was my story.

CHAPTER 2

REPORT CARD DAY

He was lying in bed, shaking. He was frightened and only ten years old. None of his friends lived like this; he knew something was wrong. He didn't remember it always being like this. Not that it had been that good, either.

God, he was beginning to feel like an adult. The pressures seemed so great all of the time. Yes, he had heard the lectures from his father; he almost knew them by heart after hearing them so many times,

"You don't know what it's like," his father would say. "Every day, I go to the office and work my ass off for you ungrateful idiots. Do you have any idea what it's like? Do you? No, obviously you don't. Why can't you help your mother out? Just a few chores to make the load a little bit easier. But no," he would bellow. "*You* can't do that, can you?"

And the answers were always the same mumbled responses in a feeble attempt of trying to defend oneself. No answer was ever quite good enough. There was a lot of stress, being a kid.

There was at least in this family.

There was even more pressure being the oldest kid. He always had to set the example for the younger ones, like Caroline did for John Kennedy, Jr. after their father was murdered. Danny remembered many a time when his father would mention the Kennedy family because Danny was conceived when Kennedy became President. Mark and Louise, who were twins, were being born on the same day that Kennedy was shot. 'Profiles In Courage' could always be found out on the coffee table, a grim reminder of their entrance into the world.

Danny always had to watch out for Mark. He and Mark got along well, though, almost better than best friends. It wasn't all that much easier being the older brother to Louise, either. He wasn't as close to Louise as he was to Mark. That was probably because Louise had her own room. With Mark, he had the nights to hold whatever conversations a ten-year-old and an eight- year-old could have. Alone in her room at night, Louise only had shadows and imaginary friends to confide in.

Danny always felt responsible for everything as the oldest. He figured it was supposed to be that way. His father always said, "You're their big brother. How are they supposed to know how to behave if you don't set a good example for them?" Of course, Danny could never come up with the right answer. There was never a right answer for Daddy. But when one of them was about to be punished, Danny always felt like he had to be there, even if he hadn't caused the problem. When they were afraid, he had to listen and he had to try and comfort them.

They were afraid a lot more often lately.

Like tonight...

It was report card night. Danny had gotten an "okay" report card and Momma didn't seem too happy about it. She kept asking why he had "B minuses" and "C plusses" instead of "A's". He had answered that he was really sorry, he had really tried. He went without dessert as punishment. It didn't bother him too much. At least he wasn't going to get the belt. Mark was going to get the belt tonight. Danny knew it as well as Mark did.

And so, Danny sat in bed, shaking, afraid and sweating.

When Momma saw Mark's report card, she warned him that he was going to get it. There had been two "D's" on it. The teacher had also written on it that Mark "plays with toy airplanes" in school instead of doing his schoolwork.

Danny looked over at Mark, who was lying in the other bed. He had to sit up because there was a dresser between the two of them. He could see him lying there with his eyes open. The dim street light cast a snow-white glow over him, which made him look faintly like a ghost. Danny could see reflections of sweat on his forehead.

"Mark?" Danny whispered.

There was no answer.

"Mark?" he whispered a little louder.

"What?" Mark answered finally.

"You okay?"

"Yeah."

"Maybe Daddy will get home late tonight," Danny offered hopefully.

"Maybe."

"If he does, he'll probably be too tired," Danny whispered.

"Maybe."

They were silent for a while. Danny could hear Momma walking around downstairs in the kitchen. He heard the clatter of pans once in a while and the opening and closing of the refrigerator door. Danny was just lying there, afraid to move. His stomach hurt and he had to go to the bathroom. It was always like this when one of them had to face the belt.

As long as he could remember, the belt had been part of their lives. Generally, it was used whenever one of the kids broke any of the Ten Commandments. As they got older though, the list of offenses which deserved the belt grew. Rough housing, talking back and any talk of sex or using a swear word could elicit the punishment. It depended upon Daddy's mood.

Both boys waited in silence.

Outside, the first winter cold front was moving in. The leafless branches of the trees began knocking against the roof as the wind picked up. The snow, which was only flurries an hour earlier, pattered thickly against the window. Nobody had to be outside to know that the temperature had dropped; ice was spreading its crystalline fingers on the windowpanes.

"I'm scared," Mark said in the darkness.

"I know. So am I," Danny answered.

"Do you think I'll get it tonight?" Mark asked.

Danny didn't answer for awhile. He listened but heard nothing but the increasing wind.

"Maybe," he answered finally.

"I wish it wasn't like this."

"So do I," Danny said in a whisper. The two of them were used to whispering softly. There had been many a time when they had been caught talking after eight o'clock. The light would snap on and then hell would ensue.

Suddenly, both of them heard the sound of the Blazer pulling up in the driveway. As the truck climbed and made traction, they waited for the lights to flash through their second story window. A moment later, they saw the lights and heard the sound of the electric garage door opening. Danny suddenly had to go to the bathroom very badly. He knew he was really scared because he had to go "number two" instead of "number one".

"He's home!" Mark said in a frantic whisper.

"Shhh!" Danny whispered back.

Danny hoped and prayed that Momma wouldn't say anything about their report cards. Maybe, just maybe, she would keep it to herself.

Moments later, they heard the laundry room door slam downstairs. They knew Daddy would be unzipping his galoshes and placing them with the other three pair on the mat in the closet.

"Hi, honey," their mother said from downstairs.

Whenever their father would come home, he would come up to the middle level where the foyer was and drop his car keys in the bureau below the foyer mirror, open the closet door and hang his overcoat in it. They heard him walk over to Momma and give her a kiss on the cheek.

"How did it go?" Momma asked him

"I guess it went okay," he answered. "You know, it never ceases to amaze me."

"What's that?"

"Oh, the innumerable ways that people destroy their mouths." Daddy was an Oral Surgeon. "This kid, seventeen years old, drove his car straight into a telephone pole. It took a good, solid six-and-a-half hours to piece his jaw back together. Damn drunkards!"

"My goodness, you must be tired," Momma said.

"I'm a bit irritable right now"

Both boys cringed at his response. That was never a good sign for them.

"What's for dinner?" Daddy asked.

"Pork chops."

"Sounds good."

The two of them walked into the kitchen. Their voices turned to mumbles. Danny thought that if Daddy was too tired, it might be a good sign. Maybe he wouldn't worry about the report cards. He knew that Mark was in the other bed hoping the same thing.

Then they heard footsteps in the hallway.

"And how was your day?" he asked Momma while she was in the kitchen.

The boys were sweating more now.

"Fine," Momma answered. "By the way, today was report card day."

The boys' hearts jumped.

"I think you should take a look at them," she suggested.

As Daddy walked back into the kitchen, Danny knew what was going on. Report card day had always been a big deal, something Danny never looked forward to. He remembered hiding his very first report card in first grade because he had been afraid of their response, and he didn't even understand what his grades meant. As it had turned out, his grades had been excellent but he had received the belt for hiding them.

Momma handed Daddy the report cards. The chair slid back from the kitchen table, making a scraping sound on the linoleum floor. Danny could picture his father settling down to inspect them.

Silence followed, except for the sounds of Momma preparing Daddy's dinner. Danny heard a kitchen drawer sliding open and the sound of silverware being placed on the glass kitchen table.

"I better talk to him about these "C's"," Daddy said in reference to the oldest son.

Fear gripped Danny. Then he heard the rustle of another envelope being opened. He could almost feel the shivers running up Mark's spine. They both knew whose card he was looking at. Daddy never bothered much over Louise's.

"What the hell kind of grades are these?" they heard him ask in a much louder tone of voice.

"I don't know what's going on with him, honey. I was thinking of calling his teacher tomorrow," Momma answered.

"We damn well better speak with his teacher," he said. "Where is he?"

Both boys knew what would happen next.

"Upstairs. Asleep."

"I'm going to have a talk with him," he said firmly. The kitchen chair scraped the floor again as he stood up.

"Honey, please!" Momma implored. "Dinner's almost ready."

"Keep it warm. I will not stand for grades like these," he said. "Mark?" he hollered from the bottom of the stairs.

Mark didn't answer, pretending he was asleep. He was hoping that Daddy would go away.

"Mark? Get down here right now, or am I going to have to come up there and get you myself? "

"Yes, I'm coming," Mark answered as he threw the sheets back and scrambled out of bed.

Danny watched him hurriedly leave the room. He saw that the back of Mark's pajamas was wet.

"What is the meaning of this?" his father's voice bellowed as Mark reached the bottom of the stairs.

"I...I don't know," Mark answered fearfully.

"I think you do know!"

"I, I..."

"I...I..." Daddy mimicked. "Well, Mark, grades like these will not be tolerated in my house! I think that it's time that you go down to the basement and drop your pants. Maybe then I can get an answer out of you!"

"No, Daddy, please!"

"I said get down there right now!"

"Honey, I wish you wouldn't," Momma interjected. "There's no need for this. Besides, you're tired."

"I'll only be a couple of minutes," Daddy responded. "Ten cracks with the belt and I'll have him back in bed."

"Okay. Only ten, though," Momma advised.

Danny heard his father come up the stairs and go past his room. He heard him rummage through the closet for his belt. Danny hoped, for Mark's sake, it would be the fat belt. The fat one hurt less than the skinny one, even though it left larger marks. Danny held his breath.

"And I'll talk to you tomorrow!" his father said to Danny, while passing his room on the way back downstairs.

He heard his father's footsteps go down the first set of carpeted stairs and then on to the tiled floor of the foyer and all the way down the next level to the basement. The sound of the basement door slamming was followed by the sound of a faint click. Danny wondered if his father had locked the door. He hoped not. He could picture what was happening next. Mark would be leaning over the tall box in the corner, where the kitty (Cookie) normally slept, and waiting for the belt.

Danny didn't know which was worse, the silence in the house now that the basement door was closed, or the noises he could imagine. Mark's whimpers, his futile pleas echoed up the stairs. "I don't want the belt, Daddy, please!" The whimpers would turn into choked cries of pain as the belt cracked down, and after the fourth or fifth crack the cries would become screams. Danny knew. He'd been there, in the basement, trying to bite back the screams of pain and humiliation. It was a losing battle.

Danny lay rigid in bed, his hands balled into fists. He tried to calculate how much time had passed, counting off the cracks, the screams, until he was sure that Mark had received the promised ten. The silence was terrifying, because he had no way of knowing what was happening.

Suddenly he heard his Momma's heels clattering down the steps to the basement, then her fists thudding on the thick door.

"Honey!" she called. "Stop it."

His father must have opened the door, because now he could hear Mark shrieking.

"He's had enough," Momma yelled.

"He'll get what he deserves. He's got to learn." Now Danny could hear the crack of the belt as it continued its' assault beyond the promised ten and he flinched each time as if it were flaying him, too. Mark's screams were thin and hopeless now, as if he didn't have the strength to protest anymore. It frightened Danny more than any other sound, and he began to cry.

It stopped as suddenly as it started.

"That'll teach you to play in school when you're supposed to be studying!" his father said in a disgusted voice. "Now pull up your pants and get out of my sight. Now!"

Danny heard the sound of Mark's feet running up the stairs, and then he was collapsing at the door to their room. He crawled to his bed, whimpering.

"Jesus, honey, didn't you get a little carried away?!" Danny heard Momma ask.

"It was a long day," Daddy answered. "I lost my temper. I'm sorry."

The wind and snow beat furiously against the window, muffling out the sound of Mark's fading whimpers.

It was a long time before Danny fell asleep.

CHAPTER 3

VICTIM OR THE CRIME

"Emergency! Emergency!" Slide down the chute!"

"He's got a snow bomb, hurry!"

Robbie and Danny looked behind them, as they were running toward the hole in the snowbank. A bundled-up figure chased them with a snowball the size of a basketball. It looked like the Abominable Snowman, with its oversized parka, black and white ski mask and frosted fur-lined face, as it ran through the snow toward them.

They jumped in a hole and disappeared. The figure chasing them tripped and fell as the snow bomb went flying. It picked itself up and dove in after them. They slid down fifty yards of the ice-packed tunnel into the gulley. They had spent weeks building the snow fort. The three of them landed in a heap in the "Control Room".

"Wow!" Danny screamed.

"That was cool!" Robbie added.

"I almost peed my pants!" giggled Mark.

The three of them watched each other's breath whistle in and out, as their heartbeats settled. The "Control Room" was the vortex of their huge underground fort. Five tunnels led to the outside world somewhere.

"Shoot," Danny said.

"What's wrong?" asked Robbie.

"We need wood. Whose turn is it?"

Mark and Robbie looked at each other. "Not ours," they said at the same time.

"No way," Danny said. "I got it last time."

Mark and Robbie both tugged a glove off.

"Ready?" Robbie asked. "On the count of three." Both of them extended their fists.

"One, two, three, GO!"

Robbie won by extending two fingers against Mark's flattened palm.

"Ha, ha, scissors cuts paper. I win," Robbie announced triumphantly.

Mark admitted defeat by crawling out a tunnel to fetch wood for the fire-pit in the center of the fort.

While waiting, Danny and Robbie talked about subjects that fascinated ten- year-olds, like combat soldiers in the far-off Vietnam war, the latest Hot Wheels (which happened to be the release of The Heavyweights) and the airplane that Daddy had just bought, a single-engine Beechcraft Debonair.

Danny had met Robbie about three years before, after seeing him sledding outside his bedroom window at about nine o'clock at night. That normally wouldn't have caused any comment, except he was sledding down Daddy's driveway and Daddy didn't like strangers on his property. Mark and Danny had already been in bed for a half hour, but Robbie had to be warned by Danny rather than by Daddy...it would be too dangerous if Daddy caught him. Danny snuck downstairs, threw on his winter coat over his pajamas and put his boots on. Well, imagine Daddy's surprise when he saw two boys sledding down his driveway an hour later. It was a friendship sealed in snow.

Mark re-appeared with the wood at Mach II, the wood flying everywhere as he careened into a frozen wall. The boys hurriedly made a fire.

"I think we're gonna move," Mark said, out of the blue.

Robbie looked up surprised, "Huh?"

"You're making up stories again," Danny said to Mark.

"Uh-uh, no way," Mark answered. "I heard Momma and Daddy talking the other night and they want to go back where they came from, now that Daddy has so much money."

"Where'd they come from?" Robbie asked.

"Detroit," Mark said dejectedly.

"I never heard that," Danny said. "I know he doesn't like it up here all that much, though. He calls everybody Yoopers."

"So what," Robbie commented. "You're gonna be Trolls now."

They bickered about five minutes over it and it was forgotten until spring when the rumor became reality.

Daddy closed his practice in Marquette, called up Allied Van Lines and, the next thing they knew, they were eating their last pasty in the Upper Peninsula and driving southward over the Mackinac Bridge to their new home in the suburbs of Detroit.

Daddy had been very successful in Marquette. He was the only oral surgeon in all of the sixteen thousand square mile area of the Upper Peninsula. When they moved to Detroit, though, Daddy had a lot of added pressure. There were many oral surgeons and he couldn't quite seem to find enough business. "I don't have enough patients," Daddy would say. He had a new three story house to pay for and there wasn't near enough money coming in.

So, Daddy was working twelve and fourteen hours a day. After a while, the pressures became too great. He was getting upset at the simplest of things.

Momma noticed, too. She decided to make sure that the kids were fed long before Daddy got home from work. She told them that Daddy was tired and would not want to put up with any of their shenanigans. Danny, Mark and Louise were learning to stay away from him when he was irritable and grouchy. They would greet him with a perfunctory "Hello, Daddy" when he got home from work and then they would dash to the safety and seclusion of their rooms. They were learning that it was best to hide from him and to say as little as possible.

Although Danny knew things were changing, there was one particular incident that served as the beginning of a number of events that would mold Danny into being the protector. In

Marquette, he had just been Danny. In Detroit, he learned to become something else. The only friend he had in Detroit was his brother. The years of whispering in bed made them very close and Detroit made them even closer. He still wasn't particularly close to his sister, Louise. Only a sissy hung around with girls too much.

One Sunday afternoon, he and Mark were playing with their gliders in the driveway. That was one thing that Daddy readily approved of. Since Daddy recently sold his Beechcraft to purchase a piper Twin Comanche airplane, he thought it would be a good idea if the boys took an interest in flying. Danny and Mark used to figure out all sorts of ways to warp the balsa wood into real aircraft which would perform high flying stunts, loop-the-loops and crash landings. For hours at a time the two boys could make their gliders go on the longest flights, the smoothest flights or the coolest flights. There was always the danger and the end of the fun when one of the planes would sail into the street where it would get crushed by a passing car.

Playing with the gliders came with every detail imaginable. The boys had to have a landing strip complete with hangars, control towers and parking lots. Hot Wheels were the perfect complement to their simulated airport. Every car imaginable could be seen scattered about in a plethora of Spectra-flame colors. They had the Twin Mill, the Splittin' Image, the Paddy Wagon, Red Baron, Whip Creamer (with the really cool fan in it that produced a whirring sound when they blew on it) finished out by the "real" looking cars like the TNT-Bird, Rolls Royce, Custom Corvette, Custom Cougar, Heavy Chevy and a classic Light-My-Firebird. The two boys could milk hours of time in a fantasy world of cars and planes.

On this particular Sunday, they came home from St. Anthony's church itching to be outside playing in the sun. They always went to ten o'clock mass on Sunday and then they were free to stay outside for the remainder of the day.

"You wanna try a take-off?" Mark asked Danny.

"How do you do that?"

"Wind up the propeller, put it on the ground and let it go," Mark answered.

"Okay."

Each boy wound up their Sleek Streaks and placed the wheels on the ground. It didn't work on the first few tries. The planes would race forward simultaneously only to flip over sideways or crash into each other. They'd pick up the planes and put them back together. Then they would warp the wings with their saliva in hopes that it would do the trick. They produced some impressive crash landings but they could never manage a successful take-off complete with a smooth landing.

"Okay, you ready?" Mark asked in anticipation of another try.

"Just a second. Let me wind it up a few more times," Danny said while twisting the little red propeller another turn or two. Finally, he squatted down next to Mark and placed his airplane about a foot away from Mark's airplane.

"Okay, Tower" Mark said, lowering his voice. "Ready for take-off."

"You ready?" Danny asked Mark in his adult voice as if they were at a real airport. Whenever Daddy would go to the airport, Danny and Mark could be seen standing at the end of the runway watching their father practicing "touch and go's". They'd pretend they were the ones in the plane instead of their father where Mark would be the pilot and Danny would get stuck being the copilot. Little did Mark know that the seed had been planted for what would turn out to be a lifelong dream.

"Just a second, let me taxi forward a little bit," Mark said while making a whirring sound with his lips. "Ready!"

The two boys let their planes go simultaneously. The buzzing sound of the propellers increased as the planes picked up speed, the little red wheels scraping the asphalt. And, to their surprise, both planes lifted into the air. Neither boy said a thing. It was too important a moment for words. They stared in awe as the planes caught the breeze and lifted higher and higher.

They couldn't believe it! They had done it! They had mastered the perfect flight!

"Get in here right now!" Momma screamed from the garage. Danny and Mark looked at each other for a moment, torn between watching the rest of their perfect flight or running in to Momma.

"Yes, Momma," they answered in unison.

"Who did this?!" she yelled accusingly. Neither boy knew what she was talking about.

"Did what?" Danny asked.

"This," she said, suddenly grabbing him by the back of the head and yanking him into the laundry room from the adjoining garage. Danny vaguely heard splashing sounds when his feet hit the laundry room floor. Mark was standing bent over, peering questioningly, while Danny was staring at the water, dumbfounded. Momma grabbed Mark by the hair and pulled him into the house and threw him against the opposite wall of the laundry room.

"Who is responsible for this?!" Momma asked them again.

"I don't know!" Danny answered, worried that Daddy might appear at any second, wondering what the commotion was about.

"Mark...?" Momma questioned.

"I don't know, either," Mark answered in a quavering voice.

"Well, somebody's lying here and I expect a truthful answer right now!"

And then Daddy appeared. When he saw the quarter-inch high water, both boys saw the angry look cross his face like the shadow of a cloud on a sunny day. They had seen the rage before, usually reserved for when one of them was receiving the belt. His lower jaw jutted forward and the muscle in his face suddenly became defined. His hands clenched into fists at his sides, the knuckles accentuated by a white tightness.

"What the hell happened here?" he shouted.

"One of the little brats left a sponge in the sink!"

Danny looked over to the sink which was actually a wash basin next to the washer. It was then that Danny realized what had happened. Mark had left the sponge in the sink when he washed his hands and the washer had been running. When the water from the washer emptied into the sink, it caused the sponge to plug up the drain, causing a minor flood.

"How many times have you been warned to never leave the sponge in the sink?" Daddy asked Danny accusingly.

"I didn't do it!" Danny answered defensively.

"Oh, you didn't?" he said, looking at Mark now. Suddenly, he reached over and grabbed Mark by the hair. "Come here, you little bastard! Do you see this? Do you?"

"Yes," Mark answered, yelping with pain.

"I don't think you do!" Daddy yelled. Danny watched in shock as his father yanked Mark off of his feet and shoved the nine-year-old boy's face into the overflowing water. Then he yanked him up just as quickly. Mark was sputtering, choking and crying.

"You don't ever learn, do you?" he said. His clenched fist backhanded Mark across the room, while Danny watched, cowering in the comer.

"I did it!" Danny blurted out. His assumed role as the protector had been born without his even realizing it.

"What?" his father asked. Mark stared at Danny, his eyes uncomprehending.

"I said that I did it. I left the sponge in the sink!"

"Are you telling me that you lied to me?" Daddy asked with a tightened face and a building rage in his eyes.

"Well, I..."

"Wasn't that a lie?"

"I, well, yes, it was," Danny answered in a high-pitched voice.

"How dare you watch your brother take the punishment that you should be getting?"

His father backhanded Danny just like he had Mark. Danny slammed into the wall, dazed. It didn't actually hurt him as much as it had shocked him. What was happening to Daddy?

"Mark, get the hell out of here! I think Danny and I have some cleaning up to do," Daddy said. Momma took the hint and left with Mark. Danny and his father were left alone.

"Get up," he demanded.

Danny stood in front of his father, trembling. If he had known what he was in for, he might never have jumped in defense of his brother. He felt himself wet his pants out of fright. His father apparently didn't notice, as Danny was already wet from the laundry room floor. Daddy struck Danny much harder.

"This will teach you not to watch your brother get punished for something you've done. Now, let's clean this up, shall we?" His wing-tipped shoes drove into Danny's shins with an unbelievable force. "That'll teach you to be dishonest with me!"

He kicked Danny again. Pain seemed to sear his legs as he fell to the wet floor. And Danny was kicked again and again. He was sure he could feel blood oozing from his legs but was afraid to look. All the while, he could hear his father's voice booming but he couldn't understand what he was saying. He was too busy trying to defend himself, warding off kicks and blows.

"I said clean it up, you sorry excuse for a son!" His father grabbed Danny by the hair and shoved his face into the floor.

Danny could feel his father putting a sponge in Danny's hand and then squeezing his hand so hard that he thought it was going to break. He had never seen his father like this and it kept on for what felt like forever, the hitting, kicking and smacking.

Then it was over. Somehow, they had gotten the laundry room clean. Danny had been beaten all the way through the task, but it was finally done. His father sent him to his room.

For a long time, Danny sat on his bed, crying and sniveling. Every bone and muscle in his body throbbed and ached. His back, legs, arms and, most of all, his scalp hurt where his father had yanked his hair so many times. Danny eventually snuck down the hallway to the bathroom. He looked in the mirror and was stunned by the sight. Bruises were beginning to show up on his face. One eye was red and Danny knew it was destined to become black. He lifted up his shirt and looked at his back. It, too, was scratched and red. After seeing it, it seemed to hurt even more. He hurried back to his room.

"Danny! I'm really sorry," Mark whispered when he walked back into the bedroom.

"It's okay. Really," Danny said.

"You shouldn't have done that."

"I don't mind," Danny said, trying to make himself believe it.

"Danny! Mark! Louise!" Momma's voice commanded. "Get downstairs and eat your dinner right now!"

The three of them hurried downstairs. Danny tried to ignore the pain as he followed his way down the steps. He walked into the kitchen and carefully pulled himself up on a stool, where the kids always ate. Momma dropped a plate of macaroni and cheese with a slice of bologna on it in front of him.

"For heaven's sake," she said. "Look at your face."

Daddy walked into the kitchen.

"Look at him," Momma said.

Daddy looked at Danny's face and turned away. "Jesus Christ," he muttered. It grew silent in the kitchen. Daddy looked at Momma and then back at Danny. "We just need to get him cleaned up. It's all superficial," he reasoned, transfixed with Danny's face. He reached over to inspect the swelling. He felt around his cheekbone and chin. "Well, nothing seems to be broken. It's just a little bruising. There's nothing to worry about."

Momma looked at Daddy accusingly.

"Goddammit," he said, returning her stare, "Just clean him up." He turned and walked out of the kitchen, running his fingers through his hair.

For the next couple of weeks, Danny's parents kept him out of school. Louise and Mark were told not to tell anyone what had happened. Neither one said a thing especially with Momma's provocation, "You can understand how difficult it is for parents, can't you?" Momma called Danny's teacher and told her he was sick with a bout of mononucleosis, he'd be out of school for a while. The teacher was very understanding and sent Danny's homework home with Mark.

During those weeks, Danny was treated very nice. His parents bought him books, gliders, models and all the Hot Wheels that he wanted. Danny loved his parents again. He knew they were sorry and that things would get better. He enjoyed life again. The only thing that he didn't particularly relish was the daily ritual of having makeup being put on his face, neck and his legs every morning.

When he finally did go back to school, he was given a note to take to his gym teacher, saying that he should be excused because of his recent illness. Danny knew it was really because the bruises and marks on his legs hadn't gone away, yet. He didn't mind, though. Danny didn't care much for gym class anyway. Besides, his parents said it was one of those fluke things and they were really sorry for what had happened.

Danny remembered the strangest thing about that incident. Particularly, it was about the two gliders that had taken off so majestically on that Sunday afternoon. He remembered the perfect take-off and wondered if they had missed the perfect landing.

Danny was saddened when Mark found the two gliders the next day, crushed in the street by a passing car. They were never able again to get two gliders to take off the way those two had.

CHAPTER 4

A SIMPLE REQUEST

"Do you want to be a doctor like your father?" Daddy would ask.

"Yes, Daddy," Danny would answer.

"Then, you're going to have to study hard."

Danny did study, a lot. It had started as far back as he could remember. Just before kindergarten, he had taken an I.Q. test. Evidently, he had done well on it, a little too well. For, while all the other kids were out playing Frisbee, baseball and all the other games that kept kids entertained, Danny was forced to sit in his room and study flashcards of arithmetic, books on penmanship and novels that Daddy deemed necessary reading for an intelligent boy. He could remember reading Black Beauty, Little Women, Tom Sawyer and a lot of Charles Dickens. He liked the reading most of all as it transformed him into a world that was very much unlike his undesirable world. Even reading Oliver Twist out loud to his brother and sister, every evening at 6:30, brought some welcome relief to a family that was becoming strained and tense.

Huckleberry Finn quickly became a favorite of Danny's. He must have read it cover to cover ten times.

In Daddy's eyes, education was a continuing process. Every waking hour of the day seemed dedicated to learning with all the kids but especially with Danny. If Danny was going to be a doctor like his father, he had a long way to go and his father was the relentless mentor. But, learning was not always fun. It could be pure hell if you wanted to really get down to it.

Just before they moved to Detroit, his father rented a Winnebago Brave, a motor home that was probably a little too small for a family of five. It was his intent to drive all the way through Canada to see Quebec, New Brunswick, Prince Edward Island and finish off the trip by seeing the largest rodeo in the world in Winnipeg, Ontario. If they had a normal family, the trip might have been fun. Unfortunately, it was the trip from hell. The better part of the days was spent driving over the great expanse of Canada in an effort to make it to the rodeo. When they would stop at night, each child was ordered to complete a "journey book" or a diary of everything they had seen and learned.

Daddy would read each of their entries in the diary out loud and then critique it. This was usually a two-hour event that ended in hair-pulling, finger-smashing and a good bout of hollering. When words weren't spelled right or sentences were worded wrong, Daddy would be sure to point them out, belittling each child as much as possible, all in the name of education.

"Without education, you're going to end up a goddamn garbage collector! Is that what you want?" Daddy would say.

The cramped quarters and the two-hour lectures eventually split up the family for part of the trip. Momma got upset when Daddy kicked Danny in the shins while they were making a campfire one night.

"Sweetheart, there was no need for that," Momma said in defense of the oldest son.

Daddy stopped what he was doing and grilled her with his eyes, "You will not teach me how to discipline our son!"

"All I'm trying to say," she said, "is that we're on vacation and we don't have to do that. Leave him alone, can't you?"

Daddy was pissed and said the hell with it and ignored Danny and Momma for a good two days while the flat landscape of Eastern Canada rolled under their wheels. The kids could not talk to each other if Momma and Daddy weren't talking. Daddy took sides with Louise and Mark while Danny stood alone with Momma. The hitting stopped, though, a blessing in disguise.

One night, while they were eating a lobster dinner on Prince Edward Island, Danny watched Momma lean over to their father and apologize for what she had done.

"All I want you to remember," Daddy said, "is that I am head of this household. Now, let's enjoy ourselves, okay?"

It was the only time that Danny had ever seen them fight. Momma knew where she stood and Daddy was happy for it.

"I love you very much," Momma said to Daddy, ending the issue once and for all.

They returned home vowing to never go to Canada again. "A waste of money," Daddy had said many times over again. "The whole country is a pigsty."

In Detroit, the incidences of punishment remained sporadic. They seemed to happen at the most unexpected times and slightly more often. Of course, Danny knew that was because the family wasn't financially on its feet yet. Daddy even had to lay off his receptionist.

Momma replaced her while the kids helped lick and stamp envelopes for bills for the few patients that Daddy did have.

Danny could see his father trying to control himself. Sometimes, when Danny thought he was in for it, his father would suddenly hold back and send him to bed. Unfortunately, it made Danny more nervous because he felt that a time would come when his father might not be able to hold back.

One day, Danny left his glasses at school. He was midway through sixth grade and had worn glasses only a short while. He hated them because all the other kids made fun of him, calling him things like "four eyes" and such. He always took them off as soon as he was out of sight from his parents.

"Where are your glasses, Danny?" Momma calmly asked him while she was fixing dinner.

Danny saw his father look up from the kitchen table. Daddy was home early because he had no patients that day. He was reading the newspaper with a sour look on his face.

"Answer your mother," his father said sternly.

"Well, I don't know," Danny answered hiding his panic trying to remember where he had left them.

"You don't know?" Daddy said with a sigh. "We spend forty dollars on new glasses so that our idiot son can see what he's doing and he doesn't know what he did with them?"

Danny stood there, not knowing what to do. It was like a test in school: the harder you tried to remember, the harder it was to think. Danny stayed silent.

"Maybe you'd like some help remembering," Daddy offered.

"No, I'll remember," Danny answered quickly. He had an idea as to what kind of help Daddy would give, especially when he was this tired. Danny's breathing sped up a little while he wrung his fingers desperately behind his back.

"Where did you leave them, Danny?" Momma piped in again.

"I'm thinking," he struggled. If he knew where he left them, they wouldn't be lost. There was no point in giving Momma and Daddy a smart-aleck answer like that. He did his best to stall for time.

"Danny?" Daddy asked, laying more pressure on him.

Did Daddy's jaw just jut forward a little bit? He had to remember...he had to.

"I'm thinking," Danny said with his eyebrows furrowed in thought. He needed just a few more seconds. Unfortunately, the more the pressure was on, the less he could remember anything save for his impending doom.

His father suddenly had enough. He stood up and took three strides toward Danny. "Maybe this will help you to remember!"

Danny backed up to the wall, as his father started poking him in the chest with his index finger. He was taunting the boy and poking him harder and harder.

"Do you remember, yet?"

"I'm trying," Danny stuttered. He tried to sidestep Daddy's prodding finger. He was thinking more about avoiding the pain than he was about the location of his stupid glasses. Danny's foot hooked on the molding, causing him to fall to the floor. Daddy reached down and grabbed him by the ankles and yanked him up in the air by his feet. Naturally, Danny started crying and screaming. There was no way he could remember now!

"Maybe you left them in your pockets, huh?"

He started shaking the boy up and down by his ankles. Danny's head was hitting the floor over and over again! He was feeling dizzy, while at the same time, he could hear his comb, pennies, gum and two Hot Wheels, the Snake and the Mongoose, dropping on the floor from his pockets. Somehow, he remembered.

"At the library! At the library!" he screamed between sobs.

Daddy dropped him back on the floor. "Very good, you little brat! How about you get your skinny little ass back to school and get them before somebody steals them!"

Danny didn't need to be told twice. He quickly picked up his stuff from the floor, scrambled to his feet and ran out the front door, grabbing his sneakers along the way. He heard his mother holler after him, "You had better be back here with those glasses or don't ever plan on coming back here at all!"

"I will," Danny answered, running down the driveway.

When he got to the street, and far enough out of sight from their house, he started walking with his hands shoved deep in his pockets. Tears were streaming down his face. He wished he never had to go back there.

A light drizzle was falling and the air was cold in the late afternoon. The remnants of winter were still around and the rain didn't make his trip any more pleasant. Danny didn't care; he was relieved to be out of the house. The rain beaded on his face, masking his tears.

For some reason, he started thinking about Huckleberry Finn and how that kid didn't have a worry in the world. Wouldn't it be cool, Danny thought, if you could just become someone else? If you got tired of your life, you'd turn your life in for someone else's like the way you change clothes for church on Sunday. Even though Huck's father was a drunk, Danny thought that he would be better than the one he had. Besides, it didn't matter to Huck Finn what kind of father he had because he just ran away.

Quite out of the blue, it hit Danny: if Huck could run away, why couldn't he? The more that Danny let the fantasy roll around in his mind, the better he liked it. Food couldn't be all that hard to find. It would be spring soon which meant that the woods would be alive with apples, berries and whatever else he could find, he reasoned. In the meantime, he would steal food from school or something like that. Any life had to be better than the one he was living. Boy, he thought, when they found out that he was gone, they'd be sorry. They might not even holler at Mark or Louise anymore if they were afraid that they'd run away too.

In spite of the drizzle, Danny began walking a little bit taller. The more he played with the thought, the more reasonable it became. Slowly but surely, Danny came to the decision that he was never going home again.

When Danny got to the school, Harry, the old, grizzly janitor let him in.

"A little early for school, aren't you?" he asked.

"I left my glasses in the library. Can I get them, Harry?" Danny asked.

"I just waxed the floors. Just be the first student here in the morning."

"Please?" Danny begged.

Harry stared at him a moment, then relented. "Alright. Do not walk on the tile. Will you do that for me?"

"Thanks, Harry!" Danny said as he ran toward the library. He heard the plop of a wet mop as Harry continued about his work.

He ran into the library and went right over to the area where the new books were stacked. He found them in the Hardy Boys section. The school felt odd with only Harry and him there.

He was about to leave the library from where he came in when he got the idea of going out the other door toward where the cafeteria was. Quickly, he pushed his way through the double doors and ran down the un-waxed hall, his shoes squeaking on the floor. He looked around twice and ran in the cafeteria. The first thing he saw was someone's windbreaker sitting over the back of a chair.

He picked it up and sized it. It might be big but it would fit, giving him some protection from the rain outside. "Empire Gas" was emblazed in white lettering on the back with a catchy phrase written underneath: "Where To Buy It". It reminded Danny of the cafe out by the airport with the red neon sign that said, "Good Eats". No matter, Danny thought, it would work as a satchel, too.

He went into the back door of the cafeteria and found everything locked except for a cabinet with a bag of Lay's Potato Chips in it and a jar of Goober Peanut Butter, with the stripe of grape jelly running through it. Without hesitation, he took them both. At the last second, he grabbed a box of wooden matches. He wrapped the coat around them and went back into the hall. He could hear Harry whistling as he mopped the floor but he couldn't see him. Danny picked the closest door and dashed out of the school, unseen.

The drizzle had stopped, which perked up Danny considerably. He shoved the peanut butter in a coat pocket, put the coat on and tucked the chips under his arm so that he wouldn't look like a kid on the run. To any casual observer, he was just a kid walking home from school. Knowing that daylight was only good for about an hour or so, he had to think of where he was going to spend his first night alone. He was actually anticipating his adventure much more than he realized.

Danny thought of the pond down by the entrance to Wood Creek Hills. He and Mark spent many Saturdays there sailing their hand-made boats and digging up duck eggs, much to the consternation of the neighboring residents. He figured that it would be a great place to hide out temporarily since one side of it was bordered by trees. In case his parents came looking for him, he didn't want to be seen from the street. Danny shivered, not from the cold, but rather from remembering Momma's warning when he left. She had practically given him the idea to begin with, he thought bemusedly.

When he reached the pond, he looked up into the weeping willow trees. Although the branches hugged the ground, offering a good hiding place, they also looked dark and eerie blowing in the slight breeze. He was scared for a moment and then regained strength at the thought that it was better than going home. He dug the Mongoose Hot Wheel out of his pocket and rolled the wheels absentmindedly with his fingers while walking into the trees. The hill sloped downward toward the pond.

As he walked up the hill, pushing the wispy branches of the trees out of his way, he thought he could hear the slow grumble of a car every once in a while. It made his head hurt as he imagined his parents angrily realizing what their son had done. Too late now, he thought. He had made a decision and he had to stick to it. The only other sound he could hear was the matted crunch of deadened leaves and pine needles as he trampled on nature's carpet.

Ahead, in the murkiness of the trees, he saw what looked like a doghouse. Danny warily approached it, thinking that it was probably a good place for a wolf to hide. He carefully set the bag of chips down by a tree, cringing at the light crackle of cellophane. He then proceeded to tip-toe up to the structure and cautiously peered inside. It was empty, except for a piece of old carpet that covered the floor. It smelled rank, but Danny figured that it would have to do until he found something better. The roof was covered in muddy clear plastic; at least he would be safe from the rain.

Danny crawled inside the house after he retrieved his chips from the tree. He lit a match to double check that he was the only occupant. A bug scurried out of sight. He maneuvered his body around so that his head was at the opening and cracked open the bag of chips, unscrewed the peanut butter and jelly and began dipping. Half an hour later, he had both Hot Wheels out, pretending that he and Mark were on a really cool adventure in their cars. He pushed away the thought that he was going to miss his brother. An hour later, the darkness falling, he fell asleep, the Snake and the Mongoose guarding the entrance to his new home.

When he awoke, he couldn't tell what time it was. All he could see was darkness except for the twinkling of the neighborhood lights off in the distance, past the pond. He rubbed his eyes and tried to get his bearings. Moments later, he realized what had awoken him. The coat did little to break the chill that was seeping in his bones. He thought about making a fire but discarded the idea because of the neighbors across the way. He would be too easily seen.

Danny started crying. When Huck Finn ran away, it sounded like a whole lot of fun, an adventure. This wasn't fun at all. As a matter of fact, it was downright scary, Danny thought. Danny hated to admit it, but he actually thought that he missed his home. Maybe it wasn't the best place in the world, but it was sure better than being crammed in a cold and damp doghouse. At home, he had a warm bed and food to eat. He also had a brother and sister that seemed pretty far away.

Danny stopped crying when an idea occurred to him. Maybe he could go back. But he couldn't go back without trying to tell his parents what was wrong. Danny crawled out of the dog house and tore a piece of plastic off the roof. He took a wooden match out of the box. He leaned toward the dim glow of the streetlights and started punching holes in the plastic with the opposite end of the match. It took the better part of an hour to painstakingly make the note. It was like connect-the-dot without having the lines to connect. Each dot was close enough that you could read the note if you held it up to the light. When he was finished, he double checked his spelling. It read:

"Dear Momma and Daddy, please don't hit and holler at us anymore. Danny."

It looked readable to him, so he decided to run home and drop it off. It seemed perfectly reasonable that he could leave the note on the front porch and then, the next night, his parents would leave him a note agreeing not to hit or holler at him, so that he would come home.

Danny walked back home, hiding whenever a car would come by.

Though his shivering stopped with walking, he was still cold right down to the bone. It didn't help when he had to hide, because the grass and weeds always got him even wetter.

It took him about forty-five minutes before he finally saw his house looming in the distance. All the lights were on, as if his parents had been waiting for him. Danny knew it would be difficult to run up the front steps, leave the note on the doormat, ring the doorbell and then take off before they saw him. But there was no other way. They would never see it on the back porch which would mean he'd freeze to death before they ever saw it. Once he started shivering again, he found the courage to make the twenty-five yard dash.

He dashed across the street and ran up the driveway, trying to avoid the blinding glare of the lights. He was aiming straight for the front porch steps when he saw his mother standing at the living room window. She had seen him! He felt like a raccoon trapped in front of Daddy's headlights, frozen in fear. It was too late for Danny to turn around. For some reason, he lost his courage and shoved the note in the bushes as he ran up the front steps.

"Danny! Danny!" His mother cried when she opened the front door.

"I'm sorry," he said as he ran into her arms.

"Where have you been?" she asked with tears running down her face. "We were so worried about you."

"I was..." Danny started to say.

"Oh, never mind," Momma said as she squeezed him close to her. "What counts is that you're okay!"

Momma got him some clean clothes and threw some hot dogs in the oven. The next thing he knew, he was eating food that tasted like manna from the gods. All the while, Daddy stayed silent.

"Why did you run away?" Daddy asked him when he had finished eating.

"I don't know," Danny answered hesitantly.

"Just tell us why."

Danny thought about it and then got up his nerve. "I was afraid," he said.

"Afraid of what?"

"Well, ever since we moved to Detroit, you get mad a lot. It seems like we get hollered at a lot and...uh," Danny said, losing his courage.

"And what?"

"We get hit a lot."

Daddy looked at him, as if he was surprised. He looked down and started picking at his fingers. The kitchen settled in silence as Daddy thought about the words he had just heard. Then, he started talking very quietly, without looking at him.

"Danny, there are some things that you won't understand until you're an adult. As a parent, I have a lot of responsibilities. I have to work very hard every day to provide this family with a good home, food on the table and a decent education, something I always didn't have. It gets very difficult sometimes, especially when you kids misbehave. But," he said with an upraised finger, "we have to discipline you so that you'll learn the right way to behave. We don't do this because we dislike you; we do it so you'll learn. We want the best for you. Do you understand?"

"A little," Danny answered.

"We'll try to be more patient. Is that a deal?"

"Yes, Daddy. It's a deal."

"Good, champ. Why don't you go to bed and get some sleep? It's been a long night."

Danny went to bed, his spirits uplifted.

It was the last time he'd ever be glad that he came home.

CHAPTER 5

MISCALCULATED RISK

Danny's alarm clock went off at 6:30 a.m.; it was a school morning. The sun beamed through the bedroom window telling him that it was going to be a beautiful day. At least it was a school day, Danny thought. After his running away, he didn't relish the thought of being in the house more than was necessary. As was becoming the usual fare, he woke up with nervous butterflies bouncing around in his stomach.

The kids had about forty-five minutes to be out of the house if they didn't want to run into their parents. They would rather hang out at the bus stop early than be in the house when they awoke. The trick was, Danny had to wake up Mark and Louise as quietly as possible. All they had to do was get dressed and eat. They were not allowed to take showers in the morning because it woke Daddy up. He was usually not very happy if he was disturbed by the kids prior to when he woke. Danny learned to ignore the other kids when they made fun of him for not taking a shower before school although he wasn't sure how they could tell, either. It wasn't as if it was something he announced.

Momma allowed them to take showers twice a week after school. Danny and Mark shared a three minute shower because Momma and Daddy didn't think it worth the money to waste water on a bunch of ungrateful kids.

As the kids got dressed, they were careful not to make even the tiniest of sounds. If you had to say something to someone, you whispered so softly that it was almost to the point of reading lips. If you walked down the hallway past Momma and Daddy's door, you tiptoed very slowly so that the floor wouldn't creak. Further, you tiptoed across the tile floor so that the thumping sounds wouldn't rouse the parents.

All this had begun when they moved to Detroit. There were many times when one of them would bump into a closet door, sneeze, cough or, at the worst, giggle and then Daddy would come stomping out of the bedroom, clad in only underwear, yelling, "You just *had* to wake me up, didn't you? I work my ass off to keep a roof over our heads and you can't even afford your father a decent night's sleep!" Then, the kids would feel like garbage and the whole day would be ruined. It was worth it to read lips than to risk his anger.

After the kids were dressed, they would creep downstairs to the kitchen. They were allowed one of three breakfasts: Corn

Flakes, Cheerio's or puffed wheat. One bowl, no more and no less, complemented with a half a teaspoon of sugar, although Danny was known to dispense more. With the cereal, the kids were allowed one glass of their milk but not Daddy's milk. Daddy drank the expensive real milk while they were only allowed powdered milk because, as the white lettering on the box advertised: one box 'MAKES TWENTY QUARTS'!

Once in a while, if Momma was in a good mood, she'd flavor the milk with a grape or cherry Kool-Aid, masking the chalky taste. If Daddy thought his milk was too old, he'd allow the kids to have it. Unfortunately, sometimes it was, greeting the back of your throat with chunks that, needless to say, would make you instantly want to throw up. If Momma noticed that, she'd be nice and throw it away where the grape flavored milk became a welcome relief. The point was: Momma and Daddy didn't want to be put in the poorhouse trying to feed the kids.

In Danny's opinion, powdered milk ranked right up there with Momma's substitute for potatoes, "Potato Buds". Sometimes Momma wouldn't stir them quite enough, or she'd add a little bit too much salt.

The one time that Danny complained about their culinary choices was the last time he complained.

After they consumed their breakfast, they took their pre-prepared lunches out of the pantry. They, too, had a ritual set in stone behind them. It was primarily why Mark started begging for food, although that's a later story.

They could expect one of four types of sandwiches, depending upon Momma's mood and the budget that week: Plain peanut butter (creamy style, no butter or jelly), bologna, pickle-pimento loaf or peanut butter with bologna (if she was in a good mood the day before).   On Mondays, they always could expect peanut butter sandwiches because they were made on Fridays and were the only sandwiches that wouldn't spoil from sitting in the pantry all weekend. They had learned never to mention that the bread became hard and the peanut butter became a dark brown, the consistency of a soft rubber. Each single sandwich was served with three animal crackers, or Vanilla Wafers, if they were on sale that week, and an apple. The thermos was filled with Kool-Aid, though, affording them an enjoyable drink.

It was no wonder that Momma bragged that she could feed three kids on sixty-eight cents a day.

When they left the house, without a confrontation with either parent, their sense of relief was incomparable.

Danny liked school for the most part. If anything, it was a welcome reprieve from his home-life as he didn't have to worry about teachers hitting and hollering at him. He felt free and relaxed for those eight hours away from home. After a long weekend at home, Mondays were the best. Fridays were the worst because of the anticipation of another dreaded long weekend at home. All day, he could expect an increasing amount of jitters to settle in before the final school bell would ring. If weekend nervousness was bad, then Christmas vacation would be worse with the thought of spending two weeks at home with Momma and Daddy. The final day before summer vacation topped them all because, well, three months at home could be almost unbearable. Danny could have sworn, at times, that he was going to get an ulcer worrying that much. He wasn't sure if kids could get one but there were times that his stomach got so knotted up that he thought he was going to die. It was hard to understand why all the other kids would scream with glee at the final summer vacation bell.

School gave Danny a chance to daydream and to read. Momma and Daddy told him that there was no reason why he couldn't be a straight "A" student. Unfortunately, that was not always the case *because* Danny loved to read. He always got a seat in the back of the class, a luxury bestowed upon him because his last name began with a "W". In the back of the class, he could read books held under his desk, propped so that the teachers couldn't see what he was doing. He had already learned everything that was being taught way back in kindergarten. To alleviate the boredom, books were his perfect escape. He read everything he could get his hands on, in part out of defiance, but mostly to escape

The Hardy Boys were his favorite because he imagined his being a part of that family. Their dad was really nice and allowed Frank and Joe to go on any adventure they wanted to. If the boys did something wrong, their dad was compassionate about it. The best part about the series was that there were so many books about them. Just as soon as he thought he had finished them all, he would discover three more mysteries.

Another one of his favorite authors was Edgar Allen Poe. He could get lost for weeks at a time in his stories, imagining the worlds of terror that were bestowed upon people. At times, he could picture the characters being members of his family. In, 'The Pit and The Pendulum', for example, he imagined his father being the man who was trapped on the table, the arc of the ax coming closer and closer until it would slice him in half.

His favorite book, though, was, 'Death Be Not Proud', by John Gunther, the story of his son dying of cancer. Danny tried to imagine what his parents would think if he suddenly got cancer. He bet they would be sorry for some of the things they had done. He could see himself in the final scene, reaching toward his father and mother and telling them not to worry. Then, the ravages of the disease would overtake him and he would expel his final breath, with all the theatrics that came with death. Danny wished there was a way that he could get cancer but, unfortunately, he couldn't get so lucky. He must have read that book fifty times; it was great meat for daydreams.

There was one problem with reading that much. Without realizing it, focusing primarily on his books began affecting his grades. The worse his home life got, the more that he could be found buried in a book. Momma and Daddy started noticing how much Danny was reading so they took all of his books away, forcing him to work on his studies. Danny found that he couldn't concentrate after a while so he increased his reading at school, out of the watchful eyes of his parents. He needed that world of fantasy desperately and he wasn't going to let them take away that one simple enjoyment.

There came a fateful day when he became a victim of his voraciousness. It was near the middle of the semester when all the teachers handed out "Progress Reports", a sort of update on how the students were doing. He did fairly well in all of his classes except for his English class with Mrs. Hamilton. He had this feeling that she didn't like him very much. He stayed away from her because he likened her to an old gray witch with her stringy hair and crackly voice. Wrinkles made little highways on her face like a roadmap to a big city while her black mascara made her eyes look dark and mean. On top of that, she had a big mole on her chin with six black hairs protruding from it.

He knew he was in trouble the moment that she called his name. He walked up to get his report and she paused before giving it to him.

"Tsk, tsk, tsk...Danny, Danny, Danny," she commented, her dark eyes staring into his. She handed him the report, nodding her head disdainfully.

Danny walked back to his desk. He could pretty well tell that he wasn't going to open the card and receive an "A" like in all his other classes. His fingers trembled as he fingered the envelope. He was worried. If he got a "C" again, he was in trouble and he knew it. He crossed his fingers, took a deep breath and held it as he pulled the green slip out of the envelope. He peeked at it out of the comer of his eye. It was at that moment that he felt his bowels sink.

Danny asked for permission to go to the bathroom and darted out of the room, his report stuffed in his back pocket. Once he got to the boys' room, he pulled it out and looked at it as if to confirm what he had really seen. A blaring "D+" stood out as if it had a neon sign attached to it. To make matters worse, she had scribbled a note on the bottom: "Danny doesn't pay attention. Danny has to be pushed!"

Nobody needed to tell him that he could look forward to the belt when he got home after Daddy saw the report. His pacing footsteps echoed off the tiled walls as he tried to figure out what he was going to do. He could not shake the queasy feeling in his stomach as he re-read the report over and over. The rest of the day, Danny did not read because he was too pre-occupied with his problem. Further, he didn't pay attention to any of his teachers as he had bigger things on his mind, like how sore he was going to be.

It was not until his last class, social studies with Mr. Peters, did he fall upon an idea. What if he never showed his parents at all? He started thinking that he could get away with it if he was really careful. The only hard part entailed affixing his father's signature on the bottom and he doubted that Mrs. Hamilton would ever notice the difference. She had never seen his father's signature, had she? If it spared him a whipping, Danny thought it was worth the risk. The best part of the plan was that Danny was the only one in middle school with the other kids being in grade school. Momma and Daddy would never have to know that they had given out progress reports.

If only it had been a "C-", he wished over and over again.

Danny's heart sunk when he saw his father's Blazer in the garage, parked next to Momma's Cadillac, when he got home from school. He nervously walked into the house, his report hidden inside the book jacket of one of his schoolbooks.

Daddy was sitting on the couch in the family room, reading a 'Flying' magazine, with a 'Police Woman' episode on the television. Daddy liked to relax by reading with the television playing softly in the background. He'd look up once in a while, get the gist of the show, and go back to reading. It was hard to understand how he did it.

When Danny walked in, Daddy looked up at him over the rim of his reading glasses.

The very first thing his father said to him was, "Well, let's take a look at your progress report."

Danny couldn't believe his father asked him that. How did he know? "We didn't get one," Danny lied, his voice as confident as he could muster up at that moment.

"Oh really?" he said. His glasses slid a notch down on his nose, exposing his eyes more clearly. He waited for Danny to respond.

Danny wasn't sure what to say, so he buried himself a little deeper by saying, "We don't get them anymore." He almost wished that he had altered the letter "D+" into a "B+", instead. It was too late now.

"You wouldn't lie to me, would you?" he asked.

"Oh, no, Daddy. I'm not lying," Danny answered with a false bravado. "You can call the teacher if you want to." He figured that there was no chance that Daddy would risk embarrassment by calling his bluff.

Danny would have died if his father went right to the phone.

Instead, Daddy looked at his son very carefully, his face expressionless but his words were slow and firm, "You had better not be lying to me or there won't be a piece of skin left on your hide after I finish with you. Is that clear?"

"Of course, Daddy," Danny answered quickly.

Daddy returned to his reading and television, which Danny took as his intimation to leave the room. As soon as he got to his room, he exhaled quietly as if he had held his breath the whole time. He noticed that his hands wouldn't stop shaking.

The next day, on the school bus, he pulled out his report and set it on his math book. He waited for the bus to stop at a traffic light before he affixed his father's signature to the bottom line. The light turned green just as he was in the middle of his father's last name. The pen scrawled erratically as Danny cursed his luck. He scrutinized it carefully and eventually accepted it as authentic.

The first thing that Mrs. Hamilton did was to pick up the progress reports. At each desk, like a sergeant on inspection of his troops, she stopped and looked at the corresponding student's reports. The room was quiet, with each kid wishing they were someplace else. As she got closer to Danny's desk, he broke out in a cold sweat, his palms reaping the rewards. His stomach felt like it had a knot in it the size of a basketball. She'll know! Danny thought. With every step closer, Danny regretted his scheme a little more.

When she finally took a stand next to him, Danny could not find the guts to look up at her as he handed her his report. He felt like her eyes were drilling into him and that she seemed to be standing there inordinately long. He kept thinking, Go away! Go away!

Instead of going away, he heard her ask him if his parents had seen the report. She hadn't asked any of the other kids that! He couldn't believe his luck.

"Yes, Mrs. Hamilton," he said in his most polite and angelic voice. His eyes averted hers.

"Is this your father's signature?" she asked, inspecting the report carefully.

Danny could feel his classmates staring at him as if he had just walked in from another planet. "Yes," he answered quietly, frightened beyond comprehension.

Mrs. Hamilton fingered the report card envelope. He could hear it ticking as her fingernail played with it.

"You're not very good at this," she stated.

"What do you mean?" Danny asked, feigning honesty.

"Since it appears that you want to continue this charade, young man, why don't you accompany me to the principal's office?"

"No, please, Mrs. Hamilton!"

She pulled Danny to his feet by the back of his collar. "Class!" she said to all the attentive eyes of the other students, "Get to your studies. I'll be back in a few minutes after I resolve this little problem. And if anyone wants to misbehave, they can sit with Danny in the principal's office. Is that understood?"

"Yes, Mrs. Hamilton," they all answered in unison. They knew who the 'chief' was of that tribe.

To the embarrassment of Danny, he was paraded out of the class by his shoulder. As soon as they got to the principal's office, she led him to an adjoining room where bookshelves adorned the walls and file cabinets stood by a desk that was clear except for a rotary black telephone.

"Sit down," she commanded. She picked up the receiver of the telephone. "What's your telephone number?" she asked.

"It's eight-two-four-five-six-zero-zero-one," Danny stuttered.

"You must think we were all born yesterday. Well, this is what God invented telephone books for," she said as she reached into a drawer.

Danny knew that he had given a fake phone number. It occurred to him that he had given one too many numbers. He wrung his hands in consternation and dread. He also had to go to the bathroom terribly bad as soon as she found the number that she was looking for.

"Mrs. Wilcox?" she said.

Pause. To Danny's furthering dismay, Momma was home.

"I was calling to find out if you had seen your son's progress report?"

Danny could have sworn that he was going to wet his pants. He picked at the green vinyl of the chair he was sitting in, avoiding any eye contact. His goose was cooked, as Grandma would say. He waited out Momma's response.

"Yes, Mrs. Wilcox, I'm Mrs. Hamilton from Calgary Middle School. It's in reference to your son, Danny. I don't believe I know Mark, yet."

Danny could picture Momma on the other end, assuming that the phone call would have been about his brother. He could imagine her surprise.

"As I was saying," Mrs. Hamilton continued, "Danny returned his progress report today and I just needed to confirm that you and your husband saw it."

Danny stared at the twitching hairs coming out of Mrs. Hamilton's mole, trying not to think about his father's warning the night before.

"Hmmm, that's what I thought. The signature did look pretty phony to me. I've been teaching for a lot of years and I'm used to their tricks. I'll be quite frank in saying that I didn't expect this out of Danny." She gave him a sneering look that didn't make Danny feel any better about his situation. "I've seen very few of them actually have the audacity to forge a parental signature."

Danny looked down to the white tiled floor as Mrs. Hamilton informed his mother of his true grades. She ended the conversation with some pleasantries and hung up the phone. She looked at Danny.

"What is wrong with you?" she asked.

"Nothing," Danny answered meekly.

"Do you understand that what you have done is despicable and underhanded? Not only did you lie to your parents, you've lied to me. I don't like lying. Do you understand that?"

Danny didn't say anything.

She leaned on the desk and looked at her student. "If your father wasn't a doctor, I'd march you into the principal's office and ask for a suspension if not an expulsion. I don't feel that you understand the seriousness of what you've done. If you were an adult, a forgery conviction means that you'll go to prison. Imagine how your parents must feel. As far as I'm concerned, you can count yourself lucky that you're not my son or you'd get a tanning of your hide that you could tell your grandchildren about," she said with a warning from her index finger. Your parents must be so ashamed of you. You are a lousy son." She stood up abruptly, her words of admonishment complete.

Danny felt like he had been slapped in the face. For a moment, he wanted to tell her the real reason he had done it. He knew that she'd probably pick up the phone and call Momma again. If only he could tell her that he didn't realize what he'd done. He'd only been trying to protect himself. As he stood up, he realized that other kids suffered like he did, considering what she had said about tanning his hide.

He hung his head all the way back to class as he followed her marching heels going click-clack all the way down the hallway. When they got back in the classroom, he could feel the eyes of all the other kids boring down on him like he was the bearded lady at the carnival or something. They couldn't care less as to what he'd done and why he'd done it, and Danny knew that.   The fact that he was humiliated in front of everyone by going to the principal's office was almost worse than the prospect of getting the belt.

Almost but not quite.

For the second day in a row, he sat there lost in another world. Would it be the skinny belt or the fat belt? Needless to say, he didn't pay attention to any of his teachers and he found no respite in 'The Hardy Boys' nor any other piece of literature. All he could do was contemplate his demise and how severe it would be.

When Danny got home from school that afternoon, things didn't happen exactly as he thought they would. Momma made him nervous by giving him the silent treatment. He could imagine what inmates on death row felt like: doomed. Just before Daddy got home, she fed him a tasteless dinner. Danny felt like it was going to be his last meal on earth. As she threw the plate in front of him, she commanded tersely, "Eat. You're going to need it!"

Danny ate alone because Momma said the other kids weren't allowed to be near him, as if forgery was contagious. He forced the food down only because he didn't want to be sitting there like a trapped animal when his father walked in. Here and there, he tried to swallow the biggest chunks of food that he could in the hope that he might choke to death, a fate better than dealing with Daddy. It was to no avail.

"Go to your room!" Momma said curtly when he had finished.

As he was walking up the steps, he heard the sound of his father's truck pulling into the driveway. He quickened his steps to his bedroom. As soon as he got there, he dropped to his knees by his bed, did the sign of the cross and started praying as hard as he could. In school, they said that if you prayed hard enough, and God was listening, he would grant anything you wanted. All Danny wanted was to make it through the evening unscathed.

He prayed hard, too, apologizing for his forging and begging not to get the belt. When he ran out of pleas, he moved into as many "Hail Mary's" and "Our Father's" as he could say. He was probably into his second or third rosary's worth of prayers when he heard his father walk into the foyer.

"And how was your day?" Momma asked, like always.

"Another lousy one," he answered tiredly. "I saw all of two patients today and I'll be damned if we think we're going to manage like that!"

"We'll manage," Momma said. "We always do."

"At this rate, I'm starting to think that we had it a hell of a lot easier in Marquette," he said, as Danny heard his car keys drop into the foyer bureau drawer.

Danny quit praying because he couldn't concentrate anymore. He completed the sign of the cross and sat on the edge of his bed, wringing his hands in nervous frustration.

"I've got some news for you," Momma said.

Danny's stomach lurched on cue.

"Oh, what's that?"

"We've got a busy little boy named Danny."

"Oh?"

"I got a call today from Danny's teacher, Mrs. Hamilton."

"Have we met her?"

"No," Momma answered. "She sounds like a very nice lady, though."

"What did she have to say?"

"Well, she asked if we had seen Danny's progress report and..."

"I thought he didn't get one," Daddy interrupted.

"Oh, it gets even better than that," Momma said, as if she enjoyed telling the story. "Not only did he get a progress report, he returned it with a signature on it. You won't believe whose signature it was."

"Don't tell me," Daddy answered as if he already knew.

Danny was wringing his hands so hard that he thought his knuckles were going to break.

"Yours," Momma answered. "Oh, one more thing. Wait until you see the grade that he got in his English class. Here, take a look at this."

Danny could hear Daddy opening the envelope. There were a few interminable moments of anticipation.

"DANNY?" his father called from downstairs.

"Yes, Daddy?"

"I think you had better march your ass down these stairs right now!"

Danny wiped his sweaty hands on his pants, looked up toward the ceiling where God was and said a final, fervent plea. He then hurried down the stairs and faced his father.

"Do you have an explanation for this?" Daddy asked.

"I'm sorry!" Danny blurted out prematurely.

"What?"

"I didn't mean to do it," Danny confessed, his voice cracking.

Daddy leaned against the kitchen counter and looked at him. "You're sorry for what?"

"Yes, Danny," Momma said with her hands on her hips, "Why don't you tell your father what you're sorry for?"

From the way everything looked, Danny knew that he was cornered. So, rather than beat around the bush, he figured it best to come clean on everything. "I got a "D" in English and I was afraid to tell you about it. I lied last night when you asked me about it and I wrote your name on the report. I'm sorry," Danny said in a high-pitched voice.

"You did what?!"

"I got a "D" in English and..."

"No, Danny," his father said, stopping him, "Let me hear that again about MY name on a progress report."

"I accidentally put your signature on it."

Daddy stared at his son with an incredulous look on his face, as if he couldn't believe what he had heard. He looked at Momma and she nodded her head in the affirmative. He looked back at Danny. "You little son of a bitch."

"I'm sorry," Danny said. "I didn't mean to do it!"

"Do you know what you've done? Do you?"

Danny took two steps back.

Daddy slammed his fist on the kitchen counter causing everything to jump, including Danny. "Not only have you gone against my wishes by getting poor grades, you have lied to me. As if that isn't enough, you forged my name! Are you a doctor? Have you earned that right to use that title? Did you go to school for fourteen years to become a doctor?"

"No," Danny said.

"You're goddamned right you didn't! And with these kinds of grades, you never will!" Daddy yelled, white foam coming out of the corner of his mouth.

Danny watched the usual begin happening. He braced himself as Daddy's jaw jutted forward and his fists clenched. Danny waited for it, expected it, and watched the first blow backhand him into the wall.

"Now! Why don't you tell me what you did again"?

"I...please don't!"

Daddy reached down and pulled Danny up with a handful of hair.

Danny's scalp screamed, as it felt like a hundred-thousand needles were piercing his head.

"That's enough, honey!" Momma suddenly interjected.

Daddy let go of Danny's head, glaring at him.

"Remember what it says in the book, 'I'm OK, You're OK'? We're learning to have patience, remember? You're tired and he's not worth it," Momma said.

He could see his father thinking about what his mother had said. He was contemplating, letting reasoning sink in. He never broke the stare from Danny's eyes, his face red with anger, as he asked Momma, "Tell me why I shouldn't punish him."

"Don't get me wrong, he should be punished."

"Tell me why I shouldn't beat him to a pulp."

"Honey, look at me," Momma said.

Daddy looked at Danny for a few seconds, as if to say, "I'll get back to you later!" He turned toward Momma.

"First of all, I don't want to be putting make-up on him for the next two weeks. Second of all, if we do that, we're running the risk of having to explain it to his teachers. We just went through this not too long ago. Finally, if you want my opinion, I think our son is very screwed up in the head. I don't hear about other kids running away from home and forging their father's signature. Do you?"

"So, what do you suggest?"

"I think he should be grounded and then we should follow the advice of that book and take him in for some counseling."

Daddy turned and looked at his cowering son.

Although Danny could tell that he didn't like the thought of it, he could also tell that Daddy was backing down to Momma's logic.

"Besides," Momma said, still trying to convince him, "you've had a hard day. We've discussed this and you promised that you wouldn't touch the kids if you were exhausted."

He turned back toward Danny and looked at him. "You make me sick to my stomach!"

Danny felt the droplets of spit hit his face, the froth dancing at the corners of his father's mouth.

"Forgery! That is MY name, not yours! Mine!" his father reiterated.

"I'm sorry!" Danny said, feeling as lucky as a kid who had found change on the street.

"Get the hell out of my sight before I change my mind!" Daddy said with an upraised backhanded stance. "And consider yourself lucky. Next time, I won't be as nice!"

Danny didn't need to be told twice. He ducked out of his father's way and ran upstairs to his room.

Later that evening, Danny was called downstairs to the family room. His mother was sitting on one of the designer couches watching 'Hawaii-Five-O' while Daddy was stretched out, reading his 'Flying' magazine. He could hear Mark and Louise playing quietly in the basement. He stood in front of his parents, his hands wringing behind his back. This felt like it was going to be a lecture session on what a terrible kid he was.

"So, have you learned anything?" Daddy asked, peering over his glasses like a far-sighted professor.

"Yes," Danny answered meekly.

"And what have you learned?"

"I learned that I shouldn't forge and lie."

"Something you weren't aware of before today?" Daddy questioned sarcastically.

"Well, I was."

"Well, sport, your mother seems to think that you have a problem. I've given this a great deal of thought and I've decided that I agree with her. So, here's what we're going to do," Daddy said, laying his magazine down.

"We're going to take you to see Father Andolini. Maybe he can straighten you out. Wouldn't you like to be straightened out?"

"I..." Danny faltered.

Daddy mimicked an answer for his son. "Yes, Daddy, I would like to be straightened out. I would like to see Father Andolini so that I can learn how NOT to forge, lie or run away. Isn't that true?"

"Well..." Danny said, not quite wanting to belittle himself some more.

"Don't you agree, Danny? You don't want to make me upset again, do you?"

"No, Daddy."

"Well?" Daddy prodded.

"Yes, I would like to see Father Andolini so that I can get my head on straight," Danny answered, praying it was said the way he thought his father would want to hear it

"Good. I bet you feel better already."

"Yes, Daddy. I feel better."

When Daddy picked up his magazine again, Danny knew it was his cue to leave as the discussion was over. As he was walking upstairs toward his bedroom, he heard his father mutter, "Time and time again, you get slapped in the face. Now, we're wondering if we have a mental case on our hands. Christ!"

"He's just a confused little boy," Momma commented.

Danny undressed himself quietly and headed toward his bed. He thought that what Daddy had said hurt him more than what his teacher had said earlier. He was twelve years old and he might be a mental case.

When he crawled under the sheets, he remembered to say a little prayer and thank God for what he had prevented. Who knows? Danny thought, maybe Father Andolini was God's way of talking to him. He hoped so.

Danny stared at the ceiling, as tears trickled down the side of his face and made the pillow damp.

Nobody heard him cry.

CHAPTER 6

PROBLEM CHILD

"Bless me, Father, for I have sinned."

"Speak up, son."

"Yes, Father," he said a little louder.

"I am ready to hear your confession."

"Yes, Father," Danny said. He tried to organize what he was going to say.

Evidently, the priest sensed that the boy needed a little prodding. "When was your last confession?"

"The last time that I went to confession was, uh, two weeks ago."

"Yes?" Father Andolini responded from the darkened screen in the confessional.

Danny could see the silhouette of the side of the priest's head, tufts of hair and a rounded crown finished off with a large nose that curved dramatically out, its size appearing enormous. "I wasn't very good," Danny hesitantly admitted.

"Don't worry, son. If you say your confession, the Lord will forgive you. Please continue."

Danny waited a minute before he started. He always felt uncomfortable saying his confession even though his parents forced them to go at least twice a month, with extra times during holidays. Danny wondered why his parents didn't feel it necessary for they themselves to go. Not that he thought his parents committed sins. They surely didn't lie or steal, or stuff like that. He figured it was probably the kids who committed all the sins.

He maneuvered himself uncomfortably in the tiny, musty room, his knees becoming cramped. He wondered what kind of horrendous crimes had been confessed over the years in that little space. He could picture murderers, thieves and a lot of little kids baring their souls to nameless clergymen. The good thing about that little room was that everything you told, remained with the priest. So, if there was something you did that Momma and Daddy didn't catch you at, at least you could clean your slate and never have to worry about their finding out. Only God and the priest knew those deep and dark secrets.

He could tell the priest anything and it would be a secret, he assured himself.

"Son?" Father Andolini prompted.

"In the last two weeks, I wasn't very good," Danny started. "I disobeyed my parents, I ran away from home, I lied about six times and I forged my father's name on a progress report," Danny repeated from memory. He had had to rehearse this scenario twenty times in front of his parents ahead of time so it probably sounded like he was a criminal in the making. He tried to dismiss how ashamed he was inside.

"Hmmm," the priest answered after a moment, "is there anything else that the Lord should know?"

"I think that's all," Danny responded.

"Let's start at the beginning, son. Why did you disobey your parents?"

"I don't know, exactly," Danny answered. "I wasn't thinking, is all."

"Are you aware of the Ten Commandments where it says, 'Honor thy mother and thy father'?"

"Yes."

"Hmm. Why did you run away from home?"

"I was afraid."

"What were you afraid of?"

Danny debated the question. He wondered if he should just go ahead and tell the priest everything. He had to tell him! Surely, a priest would protect him. He could imagine the priest, after hearing what was going on, getting somebody to watch his parents so that they'd be caught in the act. The priest would make sure that they wouldn't get hit anymore. There'd be no more pain!

Danny faltered, "Well...because...I was..."

"Was what?"

Why couldn't he just say it?!

"Ummm..." Danny started again, a war going on in his head.

Say it! Say it!

"What?" the priest queried.

"I was afraid that I'd get punished. When my dad gets mad, he gets carried away and..." Danny said, stopping.

"And what, son? This is the house of the Lord. You can speak to me," the priest said. He was leaning closer to the screen, looking larger than life.

"What do you mean when you say, carried away?"

Despite the close confines of the confessional and the implied confidentiality, Danny lost his nerve. "I didn't mean anything," Danny blurted out.

"Are you sure, son?"

"Yes, Father, I'm sure. I was just afraid of being punished."

"Well, son, your parents punish you because they want you to be the best person that you can be in God's eyes. Do you understand that?"

"Yes."

"You must try and be good for them. But, I want you to remember something," the priest said, leaning forward and lowering his tone of voice.

"If you should need anything, the House of the Lord is always open. You can see me or any priest anytime you like. We're all part of a greater family."

"I'll remember that," Danny said meekly. He felt like dirt for almost telling the priest about his parents. What was he thinking? It wasn't like they had cast him out on the street. He was sure that they loved him, wasn't he?

"Son, try to be helpful and understanding of your parents. They carry a large burden on their shoulders, much like Jesus did when he was crucified. You may not see their cross but it is very heavy. Now," the priest said, closing the matter, "I want you to say a complete rosary in repentance for your sins. Can you do that?"

"Yes, Father."

The priest ended the confession with a closing blessing and a shadowy wave of the cross.

Danny pulled the red velvet curtain aside and knelt in a pew. He made the sign of the cross and pulled out his light green, glow-in-the-dark rosary. He began belting off prayers as fast as he could.

Out of the corner of his eye, he saw Father Andolini quietly step out of the center of the confessional, genuflect and make his way toward the back of the church, where Danny's parents were standing and waiting impatiently. Danny listened until his echoing footsteps disappeared. He heard the increased crescendo of muffled voices in the back vestibule of the church.

He looked toward the crucifix at the front of the church and admired the life-sized victim hanging from it, colors of blood dripping from the feet, hands and abdomen. He looked at the thorns that gashed the skull and the magnificent size of the nails. Danny couldn't help thinking that his problems were small compared to what happened to Jesus Christ. He finished his prayers and made his way to the back of the church.

"So, don't you feel better now?" Daddy asked him.

"Yes, Daddy."

"Why don't we all go back to the rectory where we can sit down and have a little chat?" Father Andolini suggested.

Danny and his parents followed the priest outside to a small building adjacent to the church, the priest's living quarters. Father Andolini directed them to the sitting room while he went back to the kitchen to get Danny's parents some coffee. Danny had politely refused an offer of hot chocolate because Daddy always said that they didn't need handouts from strangers.

Moments later, the priest returned with a service set of coffee. "So, where would we like to start?" he asked, when everyone had served themselves.

Danny remained in a straight backed chair while his parents settled into a comfortable looking couch that one might expect in Grandma's house. The priest pushed back in a reclining chair, stretching to get the blood going.

The priest was a large man with jowls that seemed to overflow from his face. Danny thought he reminded him of a friendly Alfred Hitchcock with his balding head and errant strands of hair that were tucked behind his ears.

Danny had always like this priest. He was like an overfriendly grandfather who had an ear for a good laugh and a bellow to match. On the other hand, he was also the man who taught

Danny everything he needed to know when he received his Confirmation.

Momma volunteered first. "I think we need to start with our son, Danny."

She pointed to Danny, as if the priest wasn't sure which person the name belonged to.

"Explain."

"We're at our wits end with him. He's acting very poorly, lately. We've tried very hard to raise him well, in the eyes of the Lord, but he seems to be getting worse. He's run away from home, he's lied to us, he's..."

Daddy interrupted, "Now he's taken to forging my signature on school documents. We're at a loss here. I work very hard to provide for this family but Danny insists on behaving in a manner that just, well, it's come to the point where I'm almost embarrassed. He's a problem child."

Danny's eyes fell to the floor, ashamed.

"We don't know what to do," Momma said, her hands folded in her lap. She threw Danny a glance, as if to further conclude that he was an insurmountable problem. Danny averted his eyes. "As his parents, we've decided that he needs some religious counseling. He needs the fear of God put in him. Maybe then, he'll understand the consequences of what he's doing to himself and to this family."

Father Andolini looked over at Danny. "Let's hear from you, son. What do you think?"

"I don't know what to say," Danny said with a squirm in his seat. "I try."

"Danny," Daddy said, "If that's trying, I'd be amused to see what you'd be like when you're not trying," a sarcastic tone in his voice. "What are we expected to do with you? We provide you with everything that a growing boy could want. We..."

"Let Danny talk," the priest interjected.

"I'm sorry for what I've done," Danny said sullenly. "I won't let it happen again."

The priest leaned forward. "Listen, Danny. We're here to help you. You must tell me what's on your mind. Why have you been behaving this way?" Father Andolini prodded. "Don't worry. Just tell us what's on your mind?"

"Nothing's on my mind," Danny said. He couldn't bring himself to talk in front of his parents. He knew if he said something that they didn't approve of, the priest wouldn't be there to help him when he got home.

"Is it drugs?"

Momma looked up, shocked. "Our son would never do drugs. We're a God-fearing family! How dare you insinuate..."

"Mrs. Wilcox," the priest said, raising his hand like a referee at a baseball game. "If we're to get to the bottom of this, we have to let your son speak for himself. Let him tell us what the problem is. That's why we're here, aren't we? To get to the root of his problem?"

"The problem, Father, lies in the fact that this boy is ungrateful for the good family that he's been given," Daddy said.

"Dr. Wilcox. Will you please let the boy speak," irritation crossing the priest's face. "Now, son, is it drugs?"

"No!" Danny answered vehemently.

"Then, what is it?"

Danny looked around at the three sets of eyes that were waiting for his answer. He shifted in his chair. Looking down at the carpet, he said quietly, "Uh, I'm afraid."

"Of what, Danny?" the priest asked softly.

"Of getting punished."

"Why are you afraid of getting punished?" the priest asked, obviously looking for a particular response.

"Because they get so mad that I get hit a lot," Danny said.

At that moment, one could have heard a pin drop. Danny was surprised that he finally said it in front of someone, while Momma and Daddy couldn't believe their ears.

"Oh my God," Daddy said, shock in his voice. "Now, do you see what I mean about lying, Father? We have never laid a hand on the boy except when he deserves it. He does it time and time again. He makes up one story after another!"

"Yes, Father," Momma piped in, "we may discipline with a heavy hand but it is nothing no other parent would do." A flushed look was on her face.

"Hold on, folks! Let's all calm down," Father Andolini said. He stood up and walked toward the window, his bushy eyebrows crested in concentration.

Danny opened his mouth to retract his damning statement when his eyes caught that of his father's. His father didn't have to say anything, the eyes spoke, piercing with anger: 'If you dare say anything more, you will get a beating like you've never had before, you ungrateful son of a bitch! Just try me! You'll be the sorriest looking boy on the face of this earth!'

All was quiet as the priest began talking slowly and confidently, turning around to face them, "I detect a problem here that may be getting out of hand. The boy is obviously frightened of the repercussions of his statement. We're not here to fight things out but rather we're here to get to the root of the problem. I've got this feeling that the problem lies in how we discipline our children. There's a fine line between dispensing discipline and shall we say, physical damage? If you have to correct your son, do you use a switch or an open hand?"

Daddy shot his son a dirty look and then looked back toward the priest.

"In the most severe of cases, and it's rare, we might use the belt."

"I would suggest the use of an open hand, in the rarest of cases," the priest modified. "But, the open hand should be used more as shock value than as a weapon of punishment..."

"Wait a minute, Father," Daddy interrupted.

"Allow me to finish, Doctor. I would also suggest watching your tongue around your children. I'm not sure what is happening here except that I see fear in your son. He shouldn't be afraid of you nor should he be afraid of God. The two of you should be supporting Danny in whatever endeavors he might be going after. Sit down and talk with him. If you're upset with him, talk about it after you have calmed down. If you're not careful, this could develop into something that you may, one day, regret."

"I'm not sure what you're saying, Father, but I don't like the insinuations. Danny is the problem here, not us! Danny!" Daddy directed his attention toward him. "Tell the priest about your problem with lying. Now!"

"I lied, Father," Danny said, obediently.

"Danny, you don't have to say that. If we're to get to the bottom of this, we're..."

"I believe that we've had enough counseling for one day," Daddy interrupted. "Put your coat on, Danny. Father, I'm afraid that this isn't going to work out. What our son needs is some professional help. I don't like having these problems focused on how we discipline our child. We appreciate your efforts, but we can't do anything about his lying. If it's okay with you, I believe that the matter is settled." Daddy stood up, making it clear that the conversation was finished.

"If that's the way you feel, Dr. Wilcox, I can't say anything else. I just wanted to offer my help."

"We know you tried," Daddy said, extending his hand toward the priest's. "Let's go, honey," he said to Momma.

The three of them walked out of the rectory, said their good-byes and piled into the Cadillac, Daddy at the steering wheel. Danny looked out the window at Father Andolini, who was leaning against the rectory door with a troubled look on his face. Danny felt sorry for the priest and the attempt that he had made. It was no use. Nobody could help this family. Nobody... except maybe Danny.

Daddy waited a moment before turning the key in the ignition. He just sat there while Danny squirmed, uncomfortable and claustrophobic. His father looked in the rear-view mirror at his son. "What is your problem?" he asked.

"I don't know," Danny said.

"Is that all you can say?"

"No."

"Then, why don't you explain to your *father* what the meaning was in that stunt you pulled in there?"

"I have a problem with lying," Danny answered, in the words he thought his father wanted to hear.

"You're damn right you have a problem with lying! You're the sorriest excuse for a son that a father could ask for!"

"Honey, please!" Momma said. "The priest is watching us!"

"Please?? Jesus Christ! He's making us crazy!"

"He needs professional counseling, honey."

Daddy twisted the key in the ignition and pulled out in the road, as Momma gave a parting wave out the window toward the priest.

"Professional counseling, hah! I'm not throwing away one more dime than I have to on that brat. Besides, we'd be the laughing stock of this town and he's embarrassed us enough! We'll take care of our problems our own way, thank you!"

"That's enough, sweetheart," Momma said again.

"Won't we?" Daddy asked with a look in the rear-view mirror.

"Yes," Danny answered.

"You're damn right, we will!"

Later that night, while Danny was lying in bed, staring at the ceiling, he listened to the windows rattle as a storm front moved over the land.

It seemed a foreboding of things to come for a problem child.

CHAPTER 7

DREAM ON

"You sons of bitches! Get away from me, you bastards! Do you hear me? Stay away! I hate you!" he screamed. "I hate you! I've had it! Do you hear me?!"

Danny was awakened by a sharp jabbing in his ribs. He awoke, startled to see an angry father standing above him. He wiped the drool from his lips. He was confused and disoriented. All he could see was light shining in his room. Out of the comer of his eye, he saw Mark staring at him with a concerned look from the other bed.

Danny struggled to focus with a vague memory of a dream that he couldn't quite grasp, that he couldn't quite remember. It had something to do with gasoline. His ribs hurt as he struggled to a sitting position.

"What the hell is your problem? What were you yelling about?" his father demanded to know, as he leaned over the bed.

Danny rubbed his eyes in confusion. "I don't know," he answered, dumbfounded.

"Yes, you do! Now, what's going on?"

Danny squirmed. "I was sleeping."

"You little bastard! Stand up!" Daddy yelled. He yanked Danny out of his bed by his hair.

"I'm sorry," Danny answered, still in the cobwebs of confusion and sleep, having no idea what he was apologizing for.

"You're damn right, you're sorry! You're the sorriest thing I've seen all day! Now, what was the meaning of that?!"

As Danny struggled for a response, he saw the frightened eyes of Mark quickly look at him and close again, only pretending to be asleep. Momma appeared behind Daddy, clad in a bathrobe, looking at Danny with uncomprehending pity. For a second, Danny thought he was dreaming.

"Where did you learn that kind of language?"

Danny knew he was in trouble, but for the life of him, he couldn't figure out what for. He had been sleeping and then, suddenly, his father was yelling at him in the middle of the night. "What language? " Danny asked in a high- pitched tone of voice.

"Fine, play dumb with me!" Daddy said.

He reached over and grabbed Danny by the ear and dragged him down the hallway to the bathroom. He picked up a bar of Cameo soap and held Danny by the back of the neck. He forced it into his mouth as Danny gagged on the bitter taste. His screams were muffled by the soap as Daddy kept yanking his head back and forth, trying to force the soap in between Danny's clenching teeth. Danny felt like he was choking to death with the soap, spit and suds forcing him to gag uncontrollably. He bent over to gag, only to have his father yank his head back, the soap bar flying out of his mouth. Danny's eyes stung from the pain.

"Honey! Stop it! " Momma said, harshly. "We're doing it again. We said we'd stop this!"

"Fine!" he answered, letting go of Danny's head.

Danny stood there, weeping and coughing; the soap leaving a rank taste in his mouth.

In a much quieter tone, Daddy asked Danny again, "Where did you learn that kind of language?"

"I don't know what you're talking about," Danny repeated, wanting to spit but knowing better. For the moment, he felt safe with Momma's presence.

"Okay, stupid, I'll bite. You woke everybody up by yelling and screaming your brat head off. Now," he said with his face about two inches from Danny's, "Where have we learned words like bitch and bastard?!"

When Daddy said those words, which he rarely said, they seemed dirty and filthy.

Danny couldn't believe he had said all of those words in his sleep. Sure, at school, with the other kids around, it was cool to say those kinds of words. They seemed strong and resolute, giving him a way to fit in, although he really wasn't sure what they meant. He never intended his parents to know about them, though.

"I learned them on the bus!" Danny blurted out, his safest avenue of escape. It seemed like a good answer. If anything, it was better than the alternative of saying that he had learned them from Daddy. "Jesus Christ! The bus? I'll tell you one thing, if I ever, ever hear that language come out of your mouth again, you'll be so sorry that you'll wish you were dead! Do you understand me?"

"Yes, Daddy," he answered, still whole-heartedly confused.

"Get your little ass in bed," Daddy said, pointing toward the bedroom.

Danny hustled back to his bedroom, turned off the light and jumped into bed. He, like Mark, closed his eyes and pretended to go to sleep.

Shortly thereafter, he could hear Momma and Daddy getting ready to go back to bed. They were both abnormally quiet for what seemed like the longest time. Danny could hear drawers being opened and shut, water going at the vanity as Momma took her make-up off, and even the sound of Daddy as he took the decorative pillows off of their bed and tossed them on the floor with a muted thump.

"God damn it," Daddy said furiously.

"What is it, honey?"

"I can't believe his mouth. He learned all that from the school bus?"

"We're in Detroit, what do you expect?" Momma volunteered.

"It's not just that. It's everything. I wanted to make the best for this family. This move to Detroit was supposed to be better for us. I thought I'd be able to give the kids everything that I didn't have the luxury of getting as a kid, myself. Is it too much to ask? A nice car, a nice house and a good education shouldn't be too much to want." He yawned and then continued. "I feel like it's all falling apart."

"If you want to know my opinion," Momma said, "I think we've taken too much upon ourselves."

"Well, what other choice have we got? Bills need to be paid." Daddy asked.

Daddy had been forced to re-start his practice in Marquette by flying up there for five days a week and then flying back to Detroit on the weekend to be with the family. Unfortunately, the stress of trying to make ends meet was getting greater instead of easier.

"You knew that this would be a risk when we decided to move down here. I would've been happy staying in Marquette," Momma offered.

"Are you telling me that you would've been happier living with a bunch of uneducated Yoopers? You call that a life? Besides," Daddy said, "didn't we move here so that we could be closer to your family?"

"Don't blame this on me. Your family lives down here, too."

"Yeah, well my family is not an issue here," Daddy retorted.

"Of course, they're not. I can't help it if you haven't talked to them in ten years."

"Are you trying to start an argument?"

"No, honey," Momma said. "All I'm trying to say is that we had a better life in Marquette, regardless of the reasons we moved down here. You're gone five days a week up north, while we're struggling to keep a house that we can't afford, anymore. You come home and the kids..."

"The kids what?" Daddy asked accusingly.

"They seem to upset you. You never used to get that angry at them. You lose your temper too often."

Danny heard Daddy sigh heavily. He was hoping that this wouldn't develop into a fight like it had in the motor home. He crossed his fingers.

"Yes, I lose my temper. Do you know why? Because I get home and all you can tell me about are all the bad things that they have done while I've been gone."

"That's not true," Momma defended.

"Oh, come on. Wasn't it you who told me about the kids scavenging from the neighbor's cherry tree? How about when you heard about them digging in the school dumpster? Or was it some other wife who told me."

"There's no need to get sarcastic with me," Momma said.

Danny cringed when he heard where the conversation was headed.

Momma had told Daddy about the cherry tree and the dumpster. Danny had been embarrassed when the neighbor came over one afternoon and told Momma about their ravaging the tree for fresh cherries. It had been a combination of playing and foraging for food. As far as diving into the school dumpster, well, it was true. Danny, Mark and Louise had been dumpster diving for a good two months before somebody called Momma.

When pressed for a reason why they had done it, Danny had said they were just playing. The truth was that they had been happy to dig through old lunch bags thrown away the day before, in hopes of scoring a left-over sandwich or whatever the bags might yield. Danny was afraid to tell Momma that the fact of the matter was that they were hungry. It was half the reason that they had scoured the Randolph's cherry tree.

Of course, when Momma told Daddy about it, Daddy was tired after being gone for five days, sleeping in his office or in a recovery room. When Daddy confronted the kids about it, the usual fare in punishment happened again.

"I'm not being sarcastic," Daddy said, "I'm telling you what kind of impression you're giving me when I come home. As far as it looks to me, they lie, they steal and they disobey. They do everything they can to make us crazy. Can't they see how hard I'm working? Do other kids treat their parents the way that they treat us?"

"They don't understand, honey. Sometimes I don't understand what's happening to us. I would be glad to trade the pursuit of wealth for having a normal family back. They want it like it used to be. I want it like it used to be," Momma said, a determination in her voice. "We never take trips anymore and we rarely get to spend time together as a family. Did it ever occur to you that the reason that they do these things is because they're looking for attention? Don't you miss having a family?"

"Of course I miss it. Are you trying to say that it's my fault?"

"No, I'm not."

"You're damned right it's not my fault. It's the people down here; they don't accept us. It's the company that the kids keep. They're taking everything for granted without even attempting to understand what I'm going through."

Momma sighed. "Come to bed, sweetheart."

A teardrop slid out of Danny's eye. He felt empathy for his father and mother. Maybe they were bad kids, after all.

For some reason, Danny's dream came back to him, the one he had before he had gone into a swearing tirade. It was about a little boy who snuck his brother and sister out of the house at 3:00 in the morning. His parents had been asleep. He remembered the feel of the cool, hard tin of a gas can, as he spilled liquid throughout the house, screaming obscenities as if he wasn't afraid of waking them. He remembered the glee he had felt as he sparked a match to the liquid and the resonant whoosh as it sparked a seemingly innocuous flame in the night. He remembered their screams of terror and his feeling of elation...

"It has to stop," Danny heard his father say. "There's no getting around it. We have to do something."

"I'm right beside you," Momma said, supportively.

Danny finally fell asleep, not hearing the rest.

Two weeks later, the family found themselves eating at an expensive restaurant called Machus Red Fox. It was a restaurant that had been in the news recently. Some famous mob or union boss had disappeared there. Daddy said the guy was probably part of a Quarter Pounder at McDonald's or something now. From the moment that Daddy had announced that they were going out to eat, he knew something was up. It wasn't anyone's birthday and it wasn't a special occasion that he could think of.

"We're moving," Daddy announced after they had finished their salads course.

Danny took a sip of his strawberry soda. "Really?"

"Where to?" Louise asked excitedly.

"Back to Marquette."

"Why are we moving?" Mark asked as he fiddled with the little umbrella that came in his soda.

"For a number of reasons, Mark," Daddy answered elusively.

"What reasons?" Danny asked.

"Reasons that you don't need to be concerned with," Momma said. "Now fix your napkin on your neck. I don't want to see food on your new sweater."

The rest of the dinner was spent in virtual silence, nobody discussing the issue again. Danny felt like he was the reason that they were moving, though. He was getting older and he was not deaf. He remembered their late night conversation and knew, as the oldest brother, that he had set a bad example. But, he knew not to inquire further because his parent's business was not his business, unless they chose to involve him.

As far as Danny could tell, money was the only other reason that they were moving. With an oral surgeon on every block, it was only a matter of time before Daddy had to admit that he had no chance of getting established in Detroit whereas in Marquette, he had been the only oral surgeon in all of the Upper Peninsula. Daddy had received many a letter from patients that he had worked on, begging him to come back. This was further supported by fellow dentists who needed his services up there.

They all said that his presence was invaluable. He had been well respected there, and had made a decent living.

There were times that Danny had heard his father complain that, "the only reason they want me back is because nobody else would be stupid enough to live in such God-forsaken territory." Danny knew that his father didn't relish the thought of going back to live with a bunch of Finlanders, Yoopers and Hicks. He begrudgingly accepted the fact they were the ones who paid the bills and he surely needed to get them paid.

Danny also had a sneaking suspicion that Father Andolini had somehow had an effect on their decision to move. He knew that his parents were feeling guilty about hitting their kids so much. He also knew that his parents loved each other but he couldn't help wondering whether they still loved their kids. When they had lived in Marquette, it seemed like a wonderful world that was far away. Detroit, though, had been a nightmare in itself because when the bills were in trouble, it followed suit that the kids would be in trouble. Their parents couldn't take their frustrations out on each other, nor could they take it out on the collectors and nor could they take them out on a priest named Father Andolini. So, it was easiest to take it out on the kids. Sadly, the kids couldn't help noticing.

Because of all those reasons, Danny was optimistic about their move.

With his father re-establishing a practice, there was no reason that things weren't meant to improve. Once the bills were paid, they would have no pressure on them. Danny hoped they would have a real family again. He felt that they were moving just in time, too. Otherwise, if he didn't kill himself, he was sure that the dreams of killing his parents might come true. That was scary.

For the next few months, the family made preparations to move. A "For Sale" sign went up in front of the house. Danny heard Daddy mention that he was selling it for just over a million dollars, a figure that surprised Danny given that they were eating on a budget of sixty-eight cents a day. Twice a month, Daddy flew his family up to Marquette in the Twin Comanche so that they could see the progress that the builders were making on their new house, an identical replica of the one they had had in Detroit. The five of them would stay in a nearby motel on U.S. 41 while Daddy would go supervise the construction workers, making sure every detail was completed in the manner that he had wanted.

Daddy had decided to build their house in Shiras Hills again, only this time, they had a plot on the exclusive street called Allouez, or "Doctor's Row", as all his old friends had called it. He also picked an area where he could have a lot of land. Danny remembered a workman asking why they had wanted so much property. Momma had answered that it was because the woods were so pretty and she didn't want to see the trees cut down. Daddy added that he didn't want neighbors moving in next to them, creating an eyesore. The workman had laughed, commenting, "Must be nice, eh? You don't want any neighbors, so you buy up all of the land. I wish I had that kind of money."

Daddy gave him a strange look, muttering, "Goddamned Yooper," under his breath. Then, Daddy came out and said, laughing with a bite of sarcasm, "Yeah, well, this way, when the kids are real brats, we can take care of it and not worry about the neighbors. Know what I mean?"

The workman forced a laugh and walked away. Danny could have sworn that he had heard the man say, "Goddamned doctors, eh?" or something to that effect.

The comment had made Danny a little sick to his stomach. He wasn't in the mood for jokes like that, wondering if maybe Daddy had been serious. If he was, their moving was going to be a real letdown considering that the kids could get the shit kicked out of them and there wouldn't be a neighbor in the world that could help. It worried Danny a lot, affecting his dreams at night, mostly. He started having horribly vivid dreams about his sister bleeding, him dying and his brother running away all of the time. He kept envisioning his father grinning and bragging about his forty acres and the solitude that they were afforded.

Destiny veered forward with a neurosurgeon purchasing their house in Detroit for a million dollars even, much to Daddy's elation. The bills were paid, good-byes were said to Momma's family and their family was off to a better life. Momma and Daddy no longer were pressured by bills, which meant that the kids didn't have to be their whipping posts to vent their anger.

That's what the children were hoping for, anyway.

Three Allied Van Line trucks pulled up, their orange and black lettering sticking out like signposts: they were really moving. In a span of three days, the trucks were loaded and the cars were packed. The following three days were spent driving the long journey northward. Although Daddy complained about moving back with the Yoopers, Danny could tell that his father was optimistic about seeing an end to all their financial problems. He could even be called cheery; he acted like a normal father, the one they previously had, long ago in Marquette. He told the kids that he would teach them how to fish.

Danny and Mark could get on a baseball team and they could look forward to picnics every Sunday, he suggested optimistically.

On the trip, Danny rode with his father in the Blazer. Momma and the other kids followed in the Cadillac. Danny got to know his father a little better and found out that he actually liked him, he didn't seem afraid of him.

Danny had never really talked with his father before, not the way that he and Mark talked. It had always seemed like a quiz session between father and son where Daddy would ask a question and Danny was forced to come up with the right answer. Danny never answered what he wanted to answer. Still, the distance between them seemed to get smaller as they got closer to the Upper Peninsula. They both admired the bridge without saying a word. Before they knew it, they hit the incline of the structure. Danny looked, in awe, at the deep blue waters below.

"Look over there," Daddy said.

Danny looked where Daddy was pointing, seeing a piece of land out in the water.

"That's Mackinac Island. We'll go visit it one day. A fight between the British and the French was fought there in the 1700's. Would you like to visit it, someday?"

"Sure," Danny answered.

"By the way," Daddy said as an afterthought. "You do want to go to college, don't you?"

"Yes, Daddy."

"Do you know what you want to be?"

Danny didn't have to think about it. The last few days had felt more like a real family than it had in a long time. He was in a great mood and enjoyed his father's company immensely. So, he answered right off the top of his head.

"I want be just like you, Daddy. I want to be a doctor."

Daddy looked at his son proudly.

The family settled into their new home without a problem. The kids were registered at their new schools and, in the fall, Danny would be entering high school, while Mark and Louise were entering Bothwell middle school.

Sadly, not three days or three weeks could change, overnight, what had occurred over the previous three years. Sure, at that point in time, things could have been straightened out, but the fact is, they weren't. The sudden and erratic outbursts that had begun on a fairly infrequent basis, now turned into something that happened regularly. What was once a freak accident had turned into habit. Unfortunately, an apology wasn't going to make the family normal.

It was far too late for that.

But it didn't stop the kids from dreaming...

CHAPTER 8

BEGGAR'S BANQUET

Things had not gotten better as Danny had hoped. They got worse and worse and worse. Not in degrees, but by leaps and bounds. Danny was growing up, which meant that he was establishing a mind of his own. He was also obtaining feelings that he didn't understand, given that he was bordering his teen years. Though he tried to make sense of those conflicting feelings, it was to no avail.

It was only a few weeks after their settling in, that the problems began again. This time, they began with Mark's twin, Louise. Louise had a problem. Even though she was a twin, she had not been graced with the same intelligence level as Mark.

When the kids were registered at their new schools, they were given a test to determine their proper placement into their proper grade levels. Mark and Danny fit where they were supposed to but Louise didn't. Both parents were called into the guidance counselor's office to discuss her problem. She had been diagnosed as having a learning disability. Although she was said to have been a slow learner, she was not mentally retarded by any stretch of the imagination. To teach her, the counselors said, it would take some additional work on the part of the parents. They would have to be very patient with her.

Daddy was pretty upset about the whole situation. He immediately registered all of the kids into summer school, even though Louise was the only one who had a problem. Daddy said that he was determined not to raise a bunch of ignorant, good-for-nothing, idiot kids. Every night, when the kids got home from school, Daddy would supervise study sessions. It might have been productive except that Daddy lacked a virtue called patience. For Mark and Danny, they learned to be happy with the extra schooling as it kept them away from home during the dreaded summer months. They ignored the other kids who made fun of them because they assumed that Mark and Danny had failed their previous grade. The two boys ignored the comments that implied that the Wilcox kids were stupid.

Louise didn't mind what the other kids said. She had a naturally sweet quality about her that Daddy interpreted as signs of being a simpleton. She would smile and laugh with the other kids, having no idea of what they were saying behind her back. She just did her best to fit in and tried to learn what was requested of her.

Every night, the same routine was replayed over and over again, like that of a favorite Beatle's album. The kids would eat at

4:30 and by 4:55; were wiping their plates clean before Daddy walked in the door. Momma would pull out the three minute egg timer, at which time, all three kids had to brush their teeth until every particle of sand had fallen through the timer. If Momma knew that Daddy was going to be late, she would test their tooth brushing skills by giving them a pill that would show how much plaque they had missed, requiring them to turn over the timer again until they got it right. If they had to brush their teeth for a half hour before Momma would release them, then so be it. Usually, they were done by the second or third try.

They were expected to go to their rooms until Daddy came home and ate. There were many times that the children's mouths would salivate at the smell of pork chops, steak or fried chicken that Momma would make especially for their father. They, of course, were subjected to the same potato buds, canned peas and slice of sandwich meat. Daddy would finish eating by 6:30, at which time, study hour began with each child lined up at the kitchen counter, books open and pencils out. After each child claimed they were finished, Daddy would subsequently quiz them until their answers met to his satisfaction. Usually, Mark and Danny fared well. Louise, on the other hand, was unfailingly subjected to a battle.

"Read it out loud, Louise," Daddy would order her.

"Okay," she'd answer, a Nancy Drew book propped in her hands. "Nancy walked over to the...the...g...grok..." she'd stutter.

"What's that?"

"I don't know this word," she'd answer.

"Yes, you do. It's right in front of you. Read it!"

"...Groker...ah...gr..."

"Read it!" Daddy would repeat firmly. It always started the same way.

The harder she tried, the more that Daddy would get upset which would only proceed to slow her down even more.

"I don't know the word," she'd say, almost in tears. "I can't get it!"

"Well, hold the book open and maybe you can see what you're doing," Daddy would say.   He'd reach over her shoulders and roughly press her frail hands against the bottom of the pages. "Now, read it!"

"It's...um..." struggling to comprehend what the word might be. "Um...groker..."

"Does that make sense?" Daddy would ask sarcastically. "You idiot! Do you think that makes sense?!"

"No?" she'd answer in the tone of a question.

"What are you looking at me for? The words are in the book, not in my face!" He'd then take his fist and slam it down on Louise's small hand. She'd yell in pain while the book would inevitably fly away from her. She'd bend over, wincing, waiting for the next blow.

"Goddammit!"

Daddy would pick up the book from the floor and roughly force it into her hands. Then, he'd grab her by the back of the head and force it into the pages of the book. "Now, can you see what you're reading?!"

Louise would answer in a mumbled scream of fright while Danny and Mark would look down at their studies, pretending that their sister wasn't getting the bejesus kicked out of her, if they were unlucky enough to still be sitting there.

"You're not reading!"

"I will! I will! I will!" she'd scream, not wanting to get hit, anymore.

Danny and Mark would be as scared as she was.

"Well? I don't hear anything!" Daddy's voice would roar.

Sometimes, if she was really lucky, the word would come to her as she'd belt it out, "Grocery."

"Now, that wasn't so hard, was it?" Daddy would ask, his voice thick with sarcasm. Then, she'd do well until the next word and the whole scene would repeat itself.

Every night the same scenario replayed itself, with one subject after another. Daddy would land one blow after another, assuming that the more he hit, the more that she might be able to retain. He also liked pinching under the arms as an effective learning technique, of which all the kids had the experience of going through.

It was handy in that it caused a lot of pain but left a bare minimum of physical marks. No bruises could be seen and accidents were prevented from a fist landing in the wrong spot. The opinion was that the more pain, the better, just don't leave any marks as Momma did not want to put them in make-up every morning.

Because of those study sessions, Danny saw it wasn't going to get any better. Little by little, Danny was growing to hate his father so much that he thought murder might actually be a plausible solution. Danny felt each blow to Louise as if he were receiving them himself. He would get so frustrated, at times, that he'd go upstairs, in the privacy of his own room, and proceed to pull his own hair or slap himself as many times as he could, for lack of anything else to do. His frustrations were no longer released exclusively in his dreams, but on himself. Louise didn't understand, and it wasn't fair.

Maybe Daddy didn't understand why Louise was afflicted with her learning disability. Maybe he didn't understand that pain didn't help but rather, worsened an already regrettable situation. Maybe, he thought he could get some results.

One day, the results would be seen, results that almost ended her life.

Danny felt like he was going to explode. He despised the life that he, his brother and sister were leading. It was inevitable that he would crack. And, one day, he did, in fact, explode.

This time, the incident centered on Mark. Mark was in seventh grade, for his summer school session. Mark hated Momma's food, just as much as Danny did. He also felt, like Danny, that he never got enough to eat. He devised a little system with the food. Since one bowl of Corn flakes hardly satisfied the needs of a growing boy, he would eat his lunch on the way to school. When lunchtime came, though, he was up a creek. The children were not allowed to have money on them and that posed a problem. He resorted to begging for food from other kids. He would wait until they finished eating, and then he would come up and ask for any leftovers. It was a success if he got a partially eaten sandwich or some fruit. Regardless of the other kids poking fun at him, he continued his begging. All that mattered was a full stomach and that took precedence over pride. It usually tasted better than Momma's food, anyway. Mark tried to convince Danny to do it, but Danny had devised his own system.

Danny would steal food out of the kitchen pantry late at night, after everyone was asleep. He would sneak downstairs very quietly, head toward the kitchen and steal whatever he could without Momma's noticing. It might be a couple of pieces of bread, some crackers or some cookies. He would stuff the food in his underwear and creep down to the lower bathroom, where he could gorge himself with whatever morsels of food he'd stolen.

Fortunately, he was never caught at it

Mark didn't experience the same good fortune that Danny did. All the kids at school commented on Mark's behavior with one of the kids telling his parents about it. One night, Momma and Daddy got a phone call while the kids were eating their dinner.

"Yes, this is Dr. Wilcox," Daddy said, after a moment on the phone.

Pause.

"Do I feed my kids?" he questioned in an insulted tone of voice. "What kind of question is that?"

Mark's eyes lit up, intuitively knowing what the question was in reference to.

"Mark does what?"

Mark turned a few shades whiter.

"Look, I'm very sorry about this," Daddy said to the person on the other end. "Don't you worry, I'll get to the bottom of this and when I do, the problem will be solved. Our children are well-fed and there's no reason for that kind of behavior."

Pause.

Mark's fork was shaking involuntarily in his hand. He knew he was in for it.

"Yes, we'll take care of it. Thank you for calling," Daddy said. The phone hit the cradle in a resounding crash. Although each child was afraid to look, they could feel their father's presence behind them.

"Guess who that was?" he asked, directing his attention toward Momma, who was preparing the parents' dinner.

"Who?"

"The mother of one of Mark's school friends," he said calmly.

"And...?"

"It seems that we have a brat kid who is begging for food from the other kids. Now, who would do that?" Daddy asked, focusing in on the guilty party.

Mark did not turn around.

Daddy grabbed him by the back of the head and threw him out of the stool. Louise and Danny flinched when the stool went crashing into the kitchen table.

"What the hell is the meaning of that?!" he screamed furiously at Mark.

Mark tried to scurry away as Daddy chased him, his jaw jutted forward in anger. He caught up to Mark and tried to backhand him, but Mark ducked while Daddy's hand crashed into the wall.

"Goddammit! Come here, you little bastard!" he yelled, his frustration increased because of his throbbing hand. He grabbed Mark by the ears and literally lifted Him off of the ground and threw him to the floor. He started driving his wing-tipped shoes into Mark's body. All the while, he was screaming at his flailing son, "I'll teach you to beg! You wanna beg? Come on! Beg like you do with the other kids!"

Mark only screamed in response to Daddy's anger.

"I said beg!!" His foot went crashing into Mark's stomach.

107

Mark screamed louder.

Danny thought that he was going to die from frustration as he sat at the counter and pretended that the mayhem wasn't going on around him. He was powerless to do anything but sit there and sweat, knowing that his father would beat the shit out of him if he tried to interfere.

At the same time, Danny noticed that Momma wasn't intervening like she used to do. Ironically, that made Danny almost madder at Momma than at Daddy. It was as if she approved of what was going on.

Danny stared at his food, now cold and dry, the muscles tightening in his face. He held his breath as long as he could, hoping to pass out. He felt crummy and dirty in his powerlessness. Once again, he wished he was in the solitude of his own room. If he had been, he knew he'd be hitting himself to release the frustration. He looked over at Louise and saw tears streaming silently down her face, her attention focused on the plate that she had not touched in five minutes. It was obvious that she didn't understand what was happening except that she hurt like Danny did.

"You want to make a mockery of our family in school?! Then, why don't you show me how you beg? "

About the only begging that Mark could do, came in the form of, "Please don't! Please don't!"

"That doesn't sound like begging!" Daddy hollered, his toe ramming into Mark's shin.

Mark took the cue as best he could, "Please, can I have some food?" he asked, screaming.

"You want food?" Daddy asked.

"Yes," Mark answered like he thought he was supposed to.

Daddy yanked him off the floor by the ear and pulled him to the kitchen counter where the two other kids were still seated, but no longer eating. He took Mark's dinner and slammed the plate in front of the frightened boy. Louise and Danny kept their eyes focused downward, afraid to watch. Then, Daddy grabbed handfuls of potato buds and crammed them into Mark's mouth. One handful after another was shoved in. As he kept shoving, food fell all over the front of Mark, on the kitchen counter and on the floor. Mark was gagging and choking. Daddy pulled the hair on the back of Mark's head and tried ramming more food down Mark's unyielding throat. Mark suddenly bucked and began throwing up. Daddy let him go, watching Mark fall to the floor, retching.

"Fine, you little bastard! Go ahead and throw up all over! That will teach you to embarrass me!" he yelled at him.

Momma watched, a momentary look of concern crossing her face.

Daddy proceeded to kick him again, "Now, clean it up!"

Mark was unable to move. Daddy prepared to kick him again.

What it was that snapped in Danny, he would never know. Deep inside, anger exploded like it never had before.

"Stop it! Stop it!" he screamed at his father.

His father looked at Danny with a stunned look on his face. One would have thought that he had just kicked him in the groin.

Not to be talked back to, he backhanded Danny from across the counter. Danny flew backwards, chair and all. His head slammed into the glass table where Mark's chair had just hit, minutes before. Danny's head flashed in white-hot pain.

"Don't you EVER talk back to me", said Daddy walking steadfastly toward Danny. Danny scurried to his feet, knowing what was next. As Daddy came toward him, a grimace of anger sealed on his face, Danny dodged out of the way. He didn't stop dodging, either. He ran out of the kitchen, into the hallway and straight out the front door. He continued running, despite his father yelling after him, "You little son of a bitch! Get back here right now, before I show you what a real beating is!"

Danny kept running as hard as he could. He ran past the forty acres of land that Daddy was so proud of, past his neighbor's houses with no destination in mind but distance. Before his parents could find him in the street with the Blazer, Danny cut through a trail in the woods, behind the Ledgarten's house. He hoped that Lucy didn't see him cut through there; he wouldn't want to explain anything to the girl that he secretly had a crush on. Then Danny thought again of his father and being caught. Danny cut through the trees even faster.

Suddenly, he broke into an open area called Farmer's Field. He collapsed in the long, brown grass, his heart beating uncontrollably while his legs felt like leaden posts. As Danny looked around, he realized that he had found a haven where his father would never think to look.

Although the neighborhood kids called it Farmer's Field, there was no land being tilled and no crops being harvested. Instead, it was a grassy field which was intercut with motorcycle trails and dotted with apple trees. It was a great place for kids to play, without any adults around to ruin any childhood fantasies that might come into action.

Danny's whole body shook for twenty minutes as his lungs gasped for oxygen. Sweat dripped into his eyes. Whether it was from the trauma of witnessing what happened at home, or whether it was from the sudden rush of adrenaline that coursed through his body, Danny didn't know. All he knew was that his running was the only solution to a situation that was far beyond his control. He had run for Mark and Louise, as well as himself. The Lord only knew how long his father might have continued his assault. Danny honestly believed that if he hadn't intervened, Mark would have been killed. His role as the protector had come into play once again. He knew that, by now, his father was too preoccupied with finding Danny, rather than beating up on Mark. At least he was sufficiently distracting Daddy's attention, or so he hoped.

Danny picked himself up from the grass and began traversing the rutted motorcycle trails. As he made his way through the field, he became more determined to never step into that house again. Never! Furthermore, he never wanted to see his parents again. He left the trail and cut through the weeds to a grove of scraggly apple trees. As he reached up and plucked a green apple off the tree, he realized that he felt good, he was free from their vengeance.

He found himself a shady place to sit under a tree and bit into his apple, chewing thoughtfully, thinking about a future away from his parents. The first thing that he'd have to do was get out of Marquette altogether. He was not exactly sure how he was going to arrange that. He figured that he could try hitch-hiking but that might be risky, especially with his parents looking for him. He played with the thought of stealing a bicycle and making his way south, like Detroit, and finding a job. He would claim that his parents were dead and he was an orphan, supporting himself. Though he'd be alone, it was a better fate than going back home to try and survive through more hell.

After Danny's optimism was renewed, he decided to stay where he was for the night. The sun was dimmed considerably with a sheet of white clouds moving overhead. He piled a bunch of leaves under a tree to make a modest bed. He lay back on the crunchy leaves and stared up at the line of clouds moving overhead.

In spite of Danny's renewed outlook, the sky stared grimly back at him.

The clouds had the strange appearance of looking like an ocean that was frozen in motion, the ripples of darkness looking like the heart of waves cresting to an ominous white. They seemed oddly strange and forbidding, as if it represented a sign of times to come. Not a sound was in the air as the evening grew, save for an occasional cricket screaming in the distant field.

That night, it was deathly quiet.

The heavy silence in the air made Danny feel alone and isolated. Not that he missed his parents. That was for sure. But he missed the company of Mark and Louise. He wondered what was going to happen to them now that he was gone. Would his parents continue their charade? Would they be punished for what Danny had done? He had a feeling that the answers to those questions would be in the affirmative. How long would it take before one of them died?

He reached into his pocket and pulled out two Hot Wheels, a Bug-eye and a Peeping Bomb. He rolled them back and forth, thinking about Mark. He remembered the last time that he had run away and realized that nothing had changed. Deep inside, he didn't think that he could leave Mark and Louise alone to fend for themselves. He started to cry. Tears streamed down his face, making soft pattering sounds when they hit the leaves.

Somebody had to know what was happening. Things didn't seem right in his family. All families couldn't be like his family. If that were the case, parents wouldn't have to support kids because they would have all run away.   Robbie wasn't afraid of his mother and father.

Danny decided that when he did talk to somebody, that person would have to make sure that Danny wasn't brought back. If he had a choice, he wanted to live in a foster home with his brother and sister. Danny was the protector and the others had to be saved. If one of them died because of his parents and Danny could have prevented it, he knew he could not live with that.

He wracked his brain for an adult that he could trust. He thought of Mrs. Thill, their babysitter when Momma and daddy went out of town once a year for a vacation from the kids. He could not remember where she lived and did not know how to get there.

He wished he knew someone like Father Andolini, who was in Detroit. What about another priest? Sure, Danny thought, why not? If one priest understood then there had to be others who would feel the same way. Danny remembered the haunting look in the eyes of Father Andolini as they drove away that afternoon. He was sure that the priest would have done something about their situation if Daddy hadn't gotten so upset. This time, though, Danny would not back down. He would stick to his guns until the priest got them safely out of there.

He wiped the tears off of his face and lay back on the bed of leaves. The sky did not seem to look as insolent.

As the clouds rushed silently over, Danny fell asleep. Hours later, he was awakened by large raindrops splashing on his face.

The tree provided almost no protection from it. He saw flashes of lightning in the distance and realized that he had to find cover quickly. Judging by the darkness, Danny guessed that it was very late. He had to find shelter.

As the patter of raindrops increased so did the ferocity of the thunder. He counted the seconds after the flash of lightning to determine how far away the approaching storm was.

"One chimpanzee...two chimpanzee...three chimpanzee...four..." BOOM! He nearly jumped out of his skin as the sound reverberated across the land. There was only one thing to do and that was to run like your pants were on fire and that was what Danny did. Since he had to see a priest, he headed for St. Peter's Cathedral, about four miles away. He ran across Farmer's Field and then had to turn around and run back because he had forgotten his two Hot Wheels. He cursed his stupidity as he retraced his steps back into the woods. The rain fell with unrelenting force. Lightning traced the sky like an Etch-A-Sketch gone wild. Thunder followed, sounding as if it was shaking the ends of the earth. Water cascaded into Danny's eyes as he stumbled blindly through the wet foliage.

The thunder and lightning became so intense Danny knew that he had to find shelter immediately, or he was going to be a goner. He knew that he would never make the distance to the church without getting struck by fifty thousand volts of electricity or whatever voltage lightning had. He broke from the trees and found himself in someone's backyard.

He looked around, attempting to get his bearings. He wiped the rain from his eyes and pushed the hair back from his forehead. As the lightning flashed, he saw that a six-man tent was propped up in the back yard, its characteristic dome looking like a mosque in the periodic flashes of white light. It was probably out there to be used to camp out during the hot summer.

Danny ran toward it and unzipped the front door and dove in. Although the floor was hard, it was dry. He looked around and realized that he could not have asked for a better place to hide. It had flapped windows all the way around, which would allow Danny to see if anyone was coming. The doorway faced the woods, affording an easy escape route. As the rain hammered the canvas, Danny said a fleeting thank you to the man upstairs...it was dry.

Up until that night, Danny had loved the excitement of thunderstorms.

Yet, as nature ravaged the land with her fury, Danny was frightened to the point that he almost considered running back to the safe haven of his home.

He dismissed the thought as quickly as it had come, knowing it would have made his running away an exercise in futility. He decided that it was best to ride the storm out so he laid down in the spacious tent and tried to close his eyes, even though the noise outside was deafening. He started to shiver, his wet clothes only making it worse. Not being able to bear it any longer, he stood up and walked over to the screen door to get a look outside.

Suddenly, a burst of orange sparks showered him, as lightning kissed a cable that was evidently hanging overhead. Intense heat followed, as Danny's body was lifted into the air, to the other side of the six-man tent. He landed on his back, pain smarting up from the hardened ground. His ears were buzzing while the smell of ozone hung thick in the air. It scared the hell out of him. For a moment, he was awash with disorientation as panic rushed through his body.

He jumped to his feet, claustrophobia burying him in its weight. He hurriedly unzipped the door and ran headlong into the storm, oblivious of its fury. At first, he was going to run right up to the neighbor's house, the ones who owned the tent. He quickly dismissed that idea, being too close to home. Instead, he decided on completing his run to the church. Even though the church was a few miles away, Danny figured it worth the risk. There was no way that he would've lasted a moment longer in the tent.

He didn't know how he made the forty-five minute run to St. Peter's Cathedral without getting hit by lightning, but he made it, the steeples looming in front of him against the lightning scarred sky. He dashed up the cement steps to the large oak doors and pulled. Thankfully, they were unlocked, ready for any potential parishioner who needed the solace of the church. The doors swung closed behind him, shutting out nature's rage.

An eerie flicker cascaded the church walls from the small candles near the altar. His tennis shoes made squishing sounds as he made his way down the center aisle toward the front of the church. He found himself a pew and slid in, without forgetting to genuflect. For a long time, Danny sat there lost in thought. Eventually, the distant booming sounds faded, the storm passing.

He lay back in the pew and was instantly asleep.

He had no idea how much time had passed when he was awakened by someone pushing on his shoulders.

"Who are you?"

"Huh," Danny said, trying to shake the comfortable sleep from his eyes.

"I said, who are you?" he asked again.

He looked up and saw that it was a priest, evidently preparing for morning mass. If took Danny a moment to figure out where he was. Judging from the diffused light coming out of the windows, it was not only morning, it was cloudy out. He told the young priest his name.

"Have you been here all night?"

"Ah, no," Danny answered. Then, he reconsidered his answer. "Actually, yes."

"What are you doing here?"

"I got lost," Danny answered.

"Well, then, let's get you home."

"No!" Danny answered emphatically.

Questions of confusion were written all over the priest's face. "What?"

Danny sat up in the pew and, as much as he tried to avoid it, he cried. The priest sat down next to him and placed a comforting arm around Danny's shoulders. Danny cried and babbled for fifteen or twenty minutes, before he finally calmed down. He felt like a wimp as it seemed like he was always crying.

"Have you eaten?" the priest asked, after his sobbing had subsided.

"No."

"Well then," the priest said with an uplifting tone in his voice, "you come with me and we'll take care of that."

Danny followed the priest into the adjoining rectory. He was offered a seat in the kitchen of the rectory while the priest busily cooked a breakfast of bacon and scrambled eggs, humming softly. He watched the priest in silence. He didn't look at all like Father Andolini. This priest was young, with a full head of dark black hair. He was also dressed in normal street clothes, giving him a more youthful look without his collar. If anyone had passed the priest on the street, they probably would never have guessed that he was a priest at all.

He laid the food in front of him and Danny ate it ravenously. It sure wasn't a lousy bowl of Corn flakes. The only time he ever saw bacon and eggs was when Momma cooked them for Daddy. Danny readily accepted the glass of orange juice that was offered to him, quickly drank it, and was offered another of which Danny didn't refuse. Orange juice was a perk they never enjoyed at home. When he was finished, he sighed with adult-like contentment.

"It was pretty good, huh?"

"Sure was, Father."

"I'm Father Regan. Can I ask why you were here this morning?"

"I was lost," Danny lied.

"Danny, please..."

Danny did not know what to say or how to say it as he had lost the nerve he had had the night before. He was also having second thoughts about the plan he had devised. Why was this priest going to be different from Father Andolini? The priest patiently waited for a response. Danny finally told him that he ran away.

"Why?"

"Because...well, because..."

118

"You're having problems at home?"

Very hesitantly, with his eyes downcast, Danny said, "Because me, my brother and sister get beat up all of the time."

"Tell me about it," Father Regan prodded gently.

Danny spilled his guts. He told Father Regan about the belt and his father's temper. He told him about the day with the gliders. He dove into Mark and Louise, emphasizing that they were just as scared as he was. Finally, he told him how Daddy had made Mark throw up and still continued to kick him. All this was said between tears and anger. Danny even told him that he was so scared that he never wanted to go back.

After he was through with his account, Father Regan appeared to ponder Danny's predicament.

"I have to call your parents and let them know that you're safe," the priest finally said.

"No, please don't!"

"Everything will be fine."

"You're not going to make me go back, are you?" Danny asked, the fright obvious in his eyes.

"Not if I don't have to. Now, what's your phone number?"

"You don't believe me, do you?"

"I believe you."

"Really?"

"Trust me, Danny," Father Regan said.

He told the priest his phone number, including all the numbers, and watched as he dialed it.

"Hello, Mrs. Wilcox?"

Pause. Danny crossed his fingers.

"My name is Father Regan and I'm calling about Danny."

Danny looked to the floor, imagining her response.

"Yes, he's fine. We're both here at St. Peter's."

Pause.

"No, that won't be necessary," Father Regan said. "Actually, I'm wondering if we might come by in a little while and talk."

Danny's heart lurched at the apparent deception.

After the priest hung up the phone, Danny started to cry again. "Please don't make me go back."

"Don't worry, Danny," the priest said, squeezing Danny's shoulder. "These things take some time to straighten out. I'm trying to look out for the best of all those concerned. We just have to talk to your mother. If I'm to help you, your brother and sister, we have to get to the bottom of this."

"Do I have to stay?"

"No, you don't. You can stay with me here at the church," the priest answered.

For the first time, Danny felt that he had real hope. The priest believed him and everything would be alright. Danny was filled with confidence upon the realization that it looked like his plan was working. All he'd have to do is stand tall.

Danny and the priest drove out to the house. On the way, Simon and Garfunkel's, 'Sound of Silence', played on the radio. Danny's stomach was a wreck because of nervous anticipation. Hopefully, they wouldn't be there any longer than they had to be. As the car made its way up the long and winding driveway, Father Regan commented on the beauty of the house.

"Not really," Danny answered dryly. A beautiful house did not necessarily mean it was a beautiful family.

Just as they parked the car, Momma came running out of the house.

"Danny, I've missed you so much! We were all so worried," she said, as she hugged him. "Thank you, Father!"

"He's fine, Mrs. Wilcox."

Momma tousled Danny's hair. "He looks wonderful!"

Danny never remembered having his hair tousled by his mother.

"Why don't you come in and have some coffee?"

"That sounds good," the priest said. "Maybe we can talk."

The three of them walked in. Momma left Danny in the kitchen while she showed the house off to the priest. The priest kept commenting on the beauty of it. He saw the bird feeders in the backyard and commented that his mother was a bird watcher. For the next fifteen minutes, they talked of their common interest in birds.

"Wait a minute," Father Regan suddenly said. "Dr. Wilcox is an oral surgeon! Your husband?"

"Yes, he is," Momma said, resplendently.

"Well, I'll be. He pulled my wisdom teeth a few years back."

Big deal, Danny thought. He wasn't too thrilled with seeing Momma and Father Regan getting along as well as they were. When was he going to tell Momma that Danny and the kids weren't staying?

"Anyway," he continued, "I came into the church this morning, only to find Danny sleeping in one of the pews."

"My goodness!"

"We got to talking for a long while over breakfast."

"What did he have to say?"

Danny braced himself for the inevitable.

"Well, I'm sure you know kids," Father Regan said. "They can have pretty vivid imaginations. With his being at the border of his teenage years, they always think that the world is falling apart around him."

A look of confusion crossed Danny's face.

"How do you mean?" Momma asked, with a sidelong look at Danny.

"Oh, there's nothing to worry about. What counts is that we were able to talk and come to an understanding between us. All kids, his age, go through some sort of trauma or another. They tend to get confused about a lot of things and there's a tendency to blame it on their parents. He's at a stage where he doesn't feel loved and the only solution to that would be taking extra care to give him some attention."

"We can give him more attention," Momma said, with another look toward Danny. "His problem is that he reads too much. It gives him all sorts of crazy ideas. I'm not sure what kind of story he concocted for you, but I can bet that it was a real doozy," she said, reaching over and patting Danny's head.

She never did that, either.

Father Regan directed his attention toward Danny. "You should realize how lucky you are. There are a lot of kids around the country who are homeless. You can bet that any of them would be glad to trade places with you, considering the beautiful home that you live in. Every day, I deal with orphans, children with alcoholic parents, and even children who are born with a drug addiction. You can't know how lucky you are until you sit in their shoes."

Danny looked down at his tennis shoes. He was angry and he felt betrayed. He knew, though, that if he looked into their eyes, they would see it on his face. At that moment, he hated the priest, just as he hated the teacher. With this nice house, the birds in the backyard and Daddy's profession, who would believe the horrors that happened behind closed doors?

Danny had failed.

The two of them finished their conversation as Momma walked the priest to the front door. He stood in the open doorway and looked at Danny.

"Are you going to be okay?" he asked.

"You promised..." Danny said.

"Tsk, Tsk, tsk" Father Regan answered as he smiled and walked out.

The moment that the door shut, Momma looked at Danny, admonishment in her eyes and tone of voice, "Wait until your father gets home."

No, everything was not going to be okay.

CHAPTER 9

LITTLE VICTORY

All day, Danny thought about Momma's menacing warning, "Wait until your father gets home". His stomach was twisted in a cobweb of knots. Momma gave him a huge pile of chores to keep him busy. First, he had to clean the garage. The workbenches were washed down completely. Momma's car was then washed by hand, both inside and out. The tips of Danny's fingers were reddened by scrubbing down the huge chrome bumpers with Bon Ami, every speck of rust disappearing with his efforts. Momma scrutinized every detail wordlessly. Inspection was done silently and, if the job was done right, she would curtly hand him another chore. If it was not done right, she'd hand him the bucket, point and walk away, a stern look embracing her face. Danny knew it was in his best interest to do each job to perfection. He hoped she might pity him enough to go easy on the story with Daddy. He knew that the chances were slim but it was worth the effort.

Although Danny worked tirelessly, he found that the best way to keep his fears quelled was to pretend that he wasn't there at all. Instead, while he was scrubbing away furiously on the bumpers, he pretended that he wasn't working on a car but rather he was busily preparing a large submarine for battle. He was not a boy in a garage on an overcast day in Northern Michigan; he was really out in California as a member of the navy. He imagined himself a strong man ready to take on the world in what would surely be a perilous fight against a foreign enemy. In his mind, he knew that he may very well lose his life underwater in some distant ocean but he was not afraid. He had seen the movie, 'Gray Lady Down', and knew that the idea of sinking could be very real. Would he be strong enough to survive?

Scenarios of fear, death and torture flew through his imagination like a plethora of colors intermingling like the twisting of a kaleidoscope. He found that it passed the time and it kept his mind off the arrival of his father coming home, a thought that he did not relish. Also, it seemed like a much better thing to do than wasting his time with praying. All God ever did was to let him down.

Hours later, after raking the pounds of used sunflower seeds under Momma's birdfeeders in the backyard, he found himself picking at the reddened blisters that had formed on his hands. He looked up, only to see his father standing in the bay window of the kitchen looking back at Danny, his hands on his hips. Danny just about wet his pants with the corresponding heat flash. Danny quickly looked down, grabbed the rake and continued raking at a highly accelerated rate. His heart thudded in his chest while his forehead broke out in a cold sweat. This wasn't the movie, 'Gray Lady Down', this was home and it was much more frightening than the prospect of drowning in some unknown waters. He quickly found, that while his father was staring at him, his mind was totally incapable of jumping into that safe fantasy world.

Two hours later, Danny was surprised that neither his father nor his mother came out to get him. He was in a sort of stalemate with them, because he would rather work his fingers to the bone than go in and face them while they were testing him to see how long it would take before he gave up and went into the house. Before he knew it, the driveway was swept, the two porches were cleaned immaculately and the shrubs were weeded before dark.

Danny reluctantly took his shoes off and went into the laundry room. He kept wiping his hands on his pants but the annoying dampness clung to his palms. He listened upstairs for a sound, any sound, so that he could surmise what kind of punishment he would be receiving. The only sound that was heard was that of the central air conditioning kicking in. He walked slowly to the bottom of the landing where the foyer was, wondering if his parents were in the kitchen off to the left. Hearing nothing, he could only assume that they were upstairs in the master bedroom. He took a couple of deep breaths and tip-toed his way upstairs to the bedroom, careful not to let any creaking sounds disturb the resonant silence that seemed to hang in the air. He exhaled when he stepped into the confines of his room.

Mark was in the corner, busily putting the finishing touches on a control tower that he had assembled out of their Lego's. Small airplanes were lined up at forty-five degree angles, the completion of the airport almost done. Hot Wheels and Johnny Lightning's were parked in neat rows in the parking lots. A Heavyweight dump truck was filled with small rocks. He looked up upon seeing Danny.

"I didn't even hear you come in," Mark said.

"As long as Momma and Daddy didn't hear me," Danny whispered back. "What's going on? Am I in trouble or what?"

"I don't think so. I heard Momma and Daddy talking about two hours ago and Momma told the whole story about Father Regan. I was waiting for Daddy to run outside and grab you but he didn't."

"I wonder how come," Danny said softly. He was suspicious. He almost wished that they would do what they needed to do rather than keeping him in anticipation.

"I think you got lucky. Real lucky! I know he was pissed at you but something happened at work."

"Like what?"

"Well, like I think somebody's suing Daddy. I heard him say that they were going after seven figures which I think that Daddy thinks it's a lot of money. He pulled somebody's wisdom teeth and then they got infected later. He performed some big operation but it didn't go well." Mark attached a beacon on the tower and pushed the dump truck away as if to say that the airport was complete. "What do you think? Is this cool or what?"

"Yeah, this is a great airport" Danny said casually. "So, what's going to happen to me?"

"Oh, Daddy went into his lecture about what a bunch of rotten kids we are and then said that he's giving up on us. He looks forward to the day that we all move out. He told Momma that you're gone the very day that you turn eighteen. He'd even buy you a set of luggage for your graduation from high school. He said that will be the end of the matter and you could rot in hell as far as he was concerned. See, you're out of trouble," Mark said with a grin.

Danny sat on the edge of Mark's bed. "So, that's it? I'm not getting the tar kicked out me."

"Guess not," Mark said, ending the issue.

For the rest of the night neither one of the boys heard from their parents.

It was as if everyone had shut themselves off from each other. To Mark and Danny, they couldn't have been more pleased.

For the next few weeks, the tenseness remained at home. Conversations were short and curt with everyone doing their chores and maintaining a silent stability. School was welcome for the three children and the fear of weekends were most intense as the 3:00 school bell rang each Friday. But, the weekends dragged by in a stony silence. Daddy was pre-occupied with his lawsuit while Momma was doing her best to support him. The kids were virtually transparent in their existence, making sure that chores were done ahead of time and to perfection. It was better than the other world that they were becoming unwillingly accustomed to.

During that period, Danny and Mark got even closer than they had ever been before. They were young, curious and destined to find their own breed of trouble. For the most part, they had avoided detection. Fortunately, Momma and Daddy didn't find out about the things that could have turned out really bad.

For instance, both Mark and Danny had been fascinated with fire for a time. It was a pastime that began slowly. They would sneak out to Farmer's Field and take wooden fruit boxes out of the trash. Daddy liked blueberries on his cereal. The boys would see a container get emptied and they'd save them up until they had a few of them. On any given Saturday, once their chores were done, Momma would send them outside so that she and Daddy could get a little peace and quiet. No sooner were the boys out the door, they'd be dashing up the trail, magnifying glass in one hand, the boxes in the other. Of course, they'd dash off on Louise because they knew that Louise would probably tell on them. They would play hide and seek and when it was her turn to hide, they'd be gone. For the next hour or so, the boys would be gleeful at watching their pretend buildings being consumed by flames. Surrounding the burning building, they'd have Hot Wheels' ambulances and fire trucks around it while they would be pretending they were adults trying to contain this imminent emergency. Then, they'd reappear at home with a bewildered Louise wondering where they were.

"We were looking for you, Louise," they'd answer innocently.

Just as quickly, Louise would respond, "No, you weren't. You were tricking me again."

"We're sorry," the two boys would say, their secret fires intact.

But, they always made sure to spend at least a little time with her in retribution.

One afternoon, Mark and Danny took off down their secret trail into the woods, which was away from the front of the house, heading to their miniature cabin. The cabin was made out of twigs, much like a badly deformed Lincoln Log house. It had the main body of the house and a small attached overhang to it where they parked a few small cars. It was Danny's idea to get hold of some gasoline from the tank that Daddy kept in the garage for the boat. They half-filled a coffee can, carried it to the site of the house.

"You ever done this before?" Mark asked.

"Of course," Danny lied.

"Just burn the house part," Mark said. "Should I take the cars out of the garage?"

"Oh no, don't worry about it. They'll be fine," Danny said as he pulled the lid off the can. He poured most of the can on the house.

Mark looked nervously around, making sure that nobody would see them. "You want to light it?"

Danny handed Mark the matches. "Naw, it's your turn."

Mark looked at Danny and then at the matches. He carefully pulled one out and struck it. He waited a moment and then dropped it on their cabin.

WHOOOSH!

The fire blew to twice their height, kissing the underbrush and small trees around them. Both boys were thrown back on their butts with the force of the blast.

Within a time period of two minutes, with a lot of running and a lot of panicking, they had the fire out. Both of them knew how close they had come to getting into trouble. If Momma or Daddy had seen it, they would surely have gotten the belt.

Mark wasn't pleased about the melted blobs that were once their cars.

Another time, Mark and Danny found that plastic bags were really cool to burn. One could twist the bags around upper branches of trees, place Hot Wheels or model airplanes underneath as targets, and light the bags. Not only did the damage to the toys look really neat, the ZIPP, ZIPP, ZIPP sound of dripping plastic added to the intensity of playing with fire. When a large drip of melting plastic landed on the back of Mark's hand, they suddenly decided that burning plastic was no longer fun.

One afternoon, they met Robbie in Farmer's Field and he showed them both Cherry Bombs and firecrackers. Mark could not build models fast enough to watch them explode into a million tiny fragments. There was the time that they blew up a B-25 Mitchell and Danny could have lost an eye. Fortunately, his wearing glasses saved his life as a tail smacked against his lens. To explain the scratch to Momma, he said his glasses had fallen off while he was riding his bike. It didn't look like Momma believed him when she took him into the optometrist to get new ones. Danny did not much like fireworks after that.

For the most part, they didn't get caught. But, then there were times they did.

Danny liked to tease Mark. For instance, Danny once had a flat blue elephant-shaped eraser with the small glue-on eyes and a jiggling eyeball. One morning, for lack of anything to do with this ugly eraser, he decided that it would be hilarious if he slipped it into Mark's peanut butter sandwich. He waited until everyone was asleep when he did the deed. Unfortunately, at lunchtime, the next day, Sister Theophane happened to be standing behind Mark when he bit directly into the eraser.

Momma got a phone call within a moment after he spit it out in disgust.

When Danny got home that night, Momma walked him out to the backyard without saying a word. It was the silence and then her ripping a branch from a fir tree that he first began to get nervous. She stripped the needles off with a swipe of her bare hand. The feeling of getting whipped by it was surprisingly similar to that of being hit by the thin belt, except that it stung a little more.

He knew he deserved it.

He learned not to put erasers in his brother's sandwiches anymore. When he pulled up his pants, tears stinging his eyes and his underwear stinging the fresh wounds, Momma looked at him directly in the eyes,

"We will not be mentioning a word of this to your father. Do you understand me?"

"Yes, Momma," Danny answered.

"He's going through enough without your shenanigans making it worse. Just because he won't discipline you now doesn't mean that I won't. Is that clear?"

Danny had a few extra chores that night. He also had no dessert and went to bed early. Mark gave him dirty looks for days.

Mark did his share of things without getting caught also. There was the time that Mark took an over-extensive interest in bugs. In particular, he liked June Bugs because they were very sedate when placed in his pencil box that he took to school every day. The June bug is a large insect, much like a Beetle or Palmetto Bug. No sooner would he get to school, he'd stash the three or four bugs in his desk. He would let them out of his pencil box so that they could roam freely in his desk knowing that in darkness, they tended to remain fairly sedate. One afternoon, though, he opened his desk and they flew free.

Sister Cora was none too pleased about the ensuing ruckus that developed.

Mark was clearly busted and received his punishment.

The strange thing was, Momma repeated her performance with the fir tree branch ending with the admonition that Daddy was not to be told.

The next morning, Mark showed Danny the profuse amount welts on his backside and Danny could have sworn that they were much worse than what he had gone through.

Daddy remained aloof from the children. They could see that things were weighing heavily on his mind and knew that it was best to steer clear of him.

For the most part, Danny enjoyed being a freshman. He had a renewed sense of responsibility and enjoyed the challenges that it sometimes presented. In particular, he liked his English class. Not only could he read as much as he wanted, under the ruse that it was for school, he discovered that he enjoyed writing. His teacher, Mrs. Iverson, took a particular interest in his writing.

One day, Danny sat down and wrote a story called, "Steel and Magnets", the story of a little boy who runs away from home because he accidentally put a baseball through his parents' front window. When he ran away in the story, a thunderstorm passed through and scared the boy so much that, in the dark of the night, the rain furiously pounding, he ran back home into the welcome arms of his parents. The story bemusedly ends with the little boy pondering that going back to your parents was just like steel coming to a magnet as was only natural.

Mrs. Iverson graded it with an "A+" and had Danny read it in front of the class. He was as proud as he had ever been.

He did not plan on her calling his parents to congratulate them on her son's achievement or his father picking up the paper from school.

When Danny walked in the door, his father was seated in the living room reading his story.

"Danny, before you go upstairs," Daddy said, the work in hand, "wait a minute. I think we have something to discuss."

Danny stood nervously in front of his father. He slowly realized what Daddy was reading, while subconsciously wringing his hands behind his back. Even though the fireplace wasn't lit, it felt very warm in there suddenly. He tried to detect the reaction on his father's face but drew nothing out of it.

He knew that he was in trouble but could not surmise the extent of it. Nothing ever turned out like he had planned. He didn't plan on the 'A+' nor had he planned on the teacher's reaction. For a time, Danny thought that maybe, just maybe, his father might do as Mrs. Iverson did and congratulate him on his spelling, grammar and sentence structure. Or, would he be happy that his son was able to construct a theme? Mrs. Iverson did say that he might strongly consider becoming a writer. It was good, wasn't it?

For the first time in his life, he was able to say what he was feeling in a story.

Only his parents were not supposed to find out about it.

Danny knew very well that that story was not all fiction like everybody thought. It came pretty damn close to the truth without the bad parts.

Daddy slowly set the paper down on the coffee table, removed his glasses and stared at Danny.

Danny did not know what to say. He could read something on his father's face and he did not think it was about a warm congratulations. He squeezed his hands behind his back a little more vigorously, as Daddy stared him down.

"What the hell is the meaning of this?!"

Danny nearly jumped. "I wrote it for school and got an 'A+' on it," he answered, quickly yet defensively.

"I don't give a damn if you wrote it for the goddamned President of the United States of America! I'm not dumb. Is this some kind of joke?"

"Well, no," Danny answered meekly. What was the harm of it? He hadn't told the real story.

"Well, no," Daddy mimicked. "You want to know about sex? You want to use words like, "damn" and "screwing around"? I didn't raise you to talk like that. Swearing is forbidden in this family, in case you need to be reminded, we believe in God in this family. Do you remember who God is?"

"Yes."

"I sure hope you do. Because if you write like this again, God will make sure that you burn in hell. Is that what you want?"

"No."

"I hope not. Don't say that I didn't warn you. Now, get your ass to bed. There'll be no dinner on the dinner table for you, champ."

"Goodnight," Danny said, turning to hustle upstairs to his room.

"Oh, Danny?"

Danny turned back around.

Very slowly and methodically, Daddy picked up his glasses and put them on. He picked up Danny's story and held it toward him. Danny was reaching for it when Daddy pulled back and tore it in half and tore it in half again. He tossed them toward Danny, the pieces slowly scattering on the soft-pile carpet.

"If you think running away is cute, then how about next time making sure that it's for good?"

Danny hurriedly picked up the pieces without saying a word, his sight blurry, but determined not to let a tear fall. He dropped the pieces in the bathroom trashcan and went to bed. For a long time, he stared at the ceiling.

He had a feeling that he had won a battle, in spite of how angry his father had been. His father hadn't raised a finger to him. How could he? It was an "A+" and you couldn't argue that, could you? Maybe his father was afraid now that he knew that Danny could think. Even better, Danny felt like he had hit his father harder than his father had ever hit him.

Just think what Danny could have written. Did it make Daddy think twice?

The only thing that really bothered him before he went to sleep was Father Regan. He had let the priest trick him.

For Danny, he had been like steel coming to a magnet and that didn't feel like victory at all.

CHAPTER 10

SHATTER THE GLASS

Things twisted significantly downward the day Daddy found out that the patient who was suing him, died. Never mind the fact that his patient did not take the antibiotics that were prescribed to her, Daddy would comment furiously. It was the bloodsucking lawyers looking for a fast million bucks out of his pocket. Compound that with the fact that both the American Medical Association and The American Dental Association had opened an investigation into his private practice. He voiced his opinion all too clearly about the prospect of both financial and professional ruin, something he had worked to build all of his life.

It did not take too long for it to affect an unstable family that was already walking on needles and hanging on by the barest of threads.

Mark reacted by finding himself a paper route. He could have cared less about earning money. What mattered was that it afforded him a few more extra hours out the house. Every morning, he was out the door by 5:30 a.m., delivering a meager twenty papers in the neighborhood. He enjoyed delivering papers in the morning and in the afternoon while also taking care of collections door to door on Saturday afternoons. It gave him a few extra bucks to grab a few new Hot Wheels and some model airplanes. The more time spent away from Daddy, the better.

Only, it was not just Daddy, anymore. Momma was starting to change, too.

One Sunday morning, he got a little overly zealous as he bombed down the driveway on his ten-speed Western Flyer. He had twenty Milwaukee Journal newspapers rigged on the back of his bike. They must have weighed a good fifty pounds. He rounded the comer at the bottom of the driveway with just a hair too much lean and a little bit too much speed. The next thing he knew, all the newspapers that he had spent the last hour assembling and rigging to the back of his bike, were airborne, fluttering all over the street. A stiff breeze was blowing, complicating his already harrowing near-death accident. Before he knew it, he was on his feet, scrambling for sports sections, comics and TV guides.

Fortunately, the neighbor across the street, Dr. Pugh, a respected gynecologist, came out to assist. Both of them were fighting the breeze and grabbing every scrap of newspaper that they could find. Mark knew that he should not have gotten the neighbor involved but he volunteered and as much as Mark wanted to do it himself, the neighbor would have it no other way. Soon, they had a huge pile of mixed up papers stacked in the driveway.

Daddy had to work early that morning. He came out to the garage and decided to amble down the driveway, wondering why the garage door was open. Mark's face turned eight sheets of white when he saw Daddy. Mark looked at the neighbor who was busily helping him, as if to say, "You better go in the house."

It was too late. "Hey, Doctor Wilcox. Your boy had a little accident here."

Daddy stared at Dr. Pugh and then at Mark. "There's no need for you to help. Mark's learning the meaning of responsibility. What happened Mark?"

"I skidded on my bike and fell," he said quietly, nervously.

"I can see that."

"You know boys, Doctor. Accidents happen," Dr. Pugh volunteered.

"Not to my boys, they don't. Why don't you let us work on this? It's pretty chilly out here. There's no need for you to step into our affairs," Daddy said, a stern tone to his voice.

"Really. I don't mind. We'll have this cleared off in a jiffy. All we..."

Daddy did not let him finish. Instead, he grabbed Mark by the ear and shoved him toward the newspapers. "Now, let's get this stuff out of the man's driveway so he can enjoy some peace and quiet. Now!"

Mark started grabbing as many papers as he could while the neighbor watched, an incredulous look on his face.

Once Mark had all the papers stacked on the Wilcox driveway, Daddy proceeded to lose his temper. It was not long before Mark was sniveling and bruised.

Meanwhile, the neighbor had strolled back into his house. It may have appeared that other people's children and other people's method of discipline really wasn't his business.

Later on, after Daddy had gone to work, Mark vented his frustrations by destroying a few models, smashing a few Matchboxes and tossing his bike into a ravine.

Danny had seen the whole thing. He watched in frustration and fear. But, there was nothing he could do. He did not like smashing his stuff like Mark did, although in times of hell, he had broken one or two things of his own. One time, he tossed his metal lunchbox across the street, breaking the Thermos inside. Momma did not take too well to it. Instead, Danny took a liking toward hitting himself in the face and pulling his own hair. He tried to hurt himself as much as he could. Fortunately, the only damage he might have suffered was mentally. He always felt terrible afterwards but it seemed to have lightened the tension in his mind.

There was no one to talk to and there was no help on the way.

Daddy was becoming increasingly difficult to figure out. He went through the daily routines of being the type of father that he was but he just didn't seem all the way there at times. Danny suspected that Momma saw his increasing distances and silences. For the kids, it was good when he was silent because he stayed away from them, sometimes for days at a time. Yet, Momma's frustrations appeared to have been increasing little by little. He started noticing Momma change and he did not like what was happening.

There was terror at one level with Daddy because he was a large man. With Momma, though, it was entirely different case.

The first time that he saw that something had gone terribly wrong was a clear and warm Saturday afternoon. This time, it was Louise who suffered.

The effects of the mental and physical abuse had taken its toll on her. Imperceptibly at first, this eleven year-old girl, with her learning disability, responded to the detrimental environment in the only way she knew how.

She went inside herself. She was just as afraid of her parents as the other children in the family, but the effect of that fear was more pronounced because of her disadvantaged situation. First of all, she was a girl. Boys are raised in such a manner that they are taught to roll with the punches. Girls, on the other hand, are taught to be protected. They're raised with the idea that they're fragile and recessive. Girls were better adapted to confide in other girls, whether it be a mother or a girlfriend or a sister. Louise had none of those options. While Mark and Danny were able to whisper to each other in the deep hours of the night, Louise was in her bedroom alone, with no one. To make matters worse, her learning disability constricted her even more, leaving her confused and lonely.

Her disability required love, understanding and patience to be dealt with properly. She needed those extra steps to bolster her mental stability. With the recent death of the patient who sued, Momma and Daddy had other things on their minds. As they deteriorated, so did Louise.

She tried as hard as she could to be what her parents wanted her to be.

Day in and day out, she looked for approval in her most minor of successes. She remembered the meaning of new words. She memorized her times tables. She retained most of the capital cities of the United States.

Unfortunately, in Daddy's eyes, that was not enough. Her reading level was three years behind that of "normal". Daddy tried to get her to catch up by making her read in every single waking hour.

There was only so much that a child could study in one sitting. When children get tired, their attention span dwindles to the point where retention is almost non-existent, like an over-soaked sponge. When this happened to Louise, Daddy would become infuriated. He did not understand that he was pushing too hard. She did not understand why he was pushing so hard. He may have been able to retain something after six hours of studying, so why couldn't she? No kid of his was going to be an idiot. He had a name to uphold and if she did not want to learn, he would damn well make sure that she would want to learn. Pain seemed to be the only thing that created any results. Her learning sessions included the pulling of hair, some pinching under the arms, and the brutal slamming of her hands or her face into a book. She cried and screamed, which only caused Daddy to do it even more. Why wouldn't she learn, dammit?!

Whenever Louise was quizzed on her studies, she did her best to give the answers that Daddy was looking for. Rarely did the answer seem to be the right one. She hardly ever walked away, unscathed. In the end, or the beginning of the end, her response was only natural. Rather than risking giving answers that were wrong, it was safer not to say anything. Oftentimes, because she clammed up, Daddy would send her to bed, and to her, that was better than suffering for the torture of giving the wrong answers.

Sometimes it worked while other times were for naught. Fear was the great inhibitor of learning.

Danny watched in terror, as her method of survival backfired. Ironically, what made it even worse, was that Daddy wasn't even there. Momma was the instigator and Danny never really recovered from the incident. It probably also marked the first time that Danny realized that they had a problem that was far too big for even the protector to handle. For years afterwards, Danny would be jarred awake from a particularly vivid nightmare that had been a recreation of that same incident. Nightmares of his screaming voice reaching out were left on deaf ears in the frustration of watching his sister in terror, his hands tied behind his back.

It happened on a Saturday afternoon. The temperature was mild outside as a plethora of birds fed themselves on the sunflower seeds that Momma routinely made sure was filled in their respective feeders. Blue Jays, Cardinals, Redpolls, Evening Grosbeaks and Chickadees were frolicking in an abundance of food, chattering their daily conversations while an entirely different scenario was building inside the house. While other kids could be heard playing on the street, the Wilcox kids were inside, doing their respective chores. Each child was banished to a part of the house, with a dampened dust cloth in hand. Danny was told to clean the kitchen, while Mark was upstairs working on the bedrooms and Louise was elected to clean the foyer and the attached living room.

In silence, each child busily dusted and cleaned, hoping they would pass Momma's ensuing white-glove test. Danny was staring at the birds outside the bay window in the kitchen, wishing for release, while his hands mindlessly wiped, lost in a fantasy world light-years away.

"What are you doing, Louise?" he heard Momma ask her from the top of the stairs, overlooking the foyer.

"I'm cleaning," she answered defensively.

Danny looked over to the connecting foyer and saw her standing next to the black, wrought-iron railing that encircled the steps to the upper landing where Momma was. A damp rag hung limply in Louise' hand. Danny quickly made himself busy, in case Momma came downstairs to investigate prematurely.

"You were not cleaning," Momma said, sternly. "I was watching you. What were you doing?"

"Well, um..."

"I asked you a question. What were you doing?"

"I was dusting the railing."

"You're lying to me."

"I'm not." Louise stammered.

"Tell the truth!"

"It's true," she defended.

"You're making upset. You know how we feel about lying." Momma pursued.

"Umm..."

"I can't hear you," Momma said, threateningly. Danny could almost feel the tightness in Momma's demeanor.

"I don't know what to say," Louise responded.

Danny watched Louise as she twisted the dust cloth in her hands. He wanted to rush over and tell Louise to answer before Momma got upset. He had seen enough in Momma, lately, to know that her mood changes were no longer just minor nuances.

He wished that Louise would say something, anything to appease Momma. The tenseness grew by the second.

"Are you going to answer me?"

"I don't know what to say," Louise answered shrilly.

"Damn you!" Momma suddenly said, infuriated.

Danny heard her come stomping down the stairs. His hair stood up on the back of his neck while his stomach twisted in fear for his sister. He busied himself in a mock display of cleaning the rungs on the kitchen stools, while watching the scene develop out of the corner of his eye.

"I'm sorry," Louise said fearfully.

"For what? "

"I don't know," she answered.

"I'm going to ask you again. What were you doing?"

"I was...I don't know."

Momma suddenly slapped her full across the face. Danny cringed at the sound of her hand as it met his sister's flesh. "Will you stop saying, 'I don't know'! That is not an answer. Now, before I get upset, are you going to tell me what you were doing?!"

"Well, yes, I was..." Louise said, tears pouring down her face. "I don't know!"

"That's it!" Momma slapped her again, much harder this time. "What?"

"Um..."

Momma slapped her again, the retort echoing across the foyer. She grabbed Louise by the shoulders and began shaking the daylights out of her. "I can't hear you! What did you say?!"

The only answer that Louise gave was muffled in cries and screams of fright.

"I said answer me!"

Louise had clammed up and nothing was going to break into that shell. Momma released her shoulders and reached back and slapped her again. Louise fell to the floor, holding her stinging face.

Danny looked on, incredulous. He had never seen Momma quite like this.

Though he had grown angry and frustrated, he didn't know what anger was until he saw what happened next.

Momma grabbed Louise' head and pushed it to the floor. "Don't you fight me, you insolent little idiot!" she screamed, while Louise squirmed in what little defense she had. Momma kicked her swiftly in the legs. Louise screamed even louder, not knowing what was going to happen next. She was now lying on her back, on the white tiled floor, while Momma towered over her.

"Are you going to answer me!'

Louise responded in a wail of fear.

"Fine. I'll get an answer out of you if it kills me. I won't be as patient as your father has been!" Momma took her foot and placed it squarely on Louise' chest. "One last chance!"

In bewilderment, Louise wailed.

With one hand holding onto the railing, Momma placed her weight on her daughter's chest. Danny heard the air rush out of Louise's lungs. After a moment or two, she stepped off of her. "Are you ready to answer me?!"

Louise only screamed louder. Momma promptly stood on her again.

She stepped off, and then stood on Louise several more times, while continuing her screaming tirade.

As this was happening, Danny watched, his eyes widened in terror. He began pinching himself as hard as he could, ignorant of the blood that he was drawing from the back of his own hand. Unknown to him, at the time, Mark was simultaneously crouched in his room, hitting himself as hard as could.

While Louise continued screaming, Momma continued to repeatedly step on her.

Danny could no longer block the screams out of his head. The pain he was rendering to himself was nothing compared to the pain of what he was watching. If Danny did not do something, he was sure that it would never end until her ribs broke. Somehow, in the ongoing madness, he saw the telephone. It seemed to be beckoning him. He would have to call the police. There was no other way around it. He hoped they would be able to hear what was happening, and they could stop it! He could not watch anymore! If only he was strong enough to fight his mother!

The telephone loomed only feet away, a potential lifeline to safety.

Louise continued screaming.

Danny had to do it! The phone...if only he could pick it up. Although only ten feet away, at the most, how was he going to get past the doorway without Momma seeing him?! As Louise screamed, he forced himself to stand and take the first step.

What if Momma saw him?

Thoughts rifled through his head. If Momma caught him, he would surely face a fate worse than what Louise was enduring. Worse yet, what if Momma actually caught him on the phone? If she was angry now, imagine her mood as she caught him mid-sentence to the police! She would kill him; there was no question about that!

There was no ignoring the fact that with each passing moment, she was killing Louise right then!

Danny panicked and rushed over to the sink, discarding any thoughts of the telephone. He grabbed the dirty glasses that were lined up, ready for him to wash. With a sweep of the arm, he pushed them to the floor. They shattered everywhere, as Danny stood there in frozen concentration.

The screaming stopped.

"What the hell is going on here?" Momma questioned as she stormed into the kitchen after Danny.

"I'm sorry! I bumped the glasses. I didn't mean to do it!" Danny lied in a terrorized voice.

"You clumsy brat! Clean it up or shall I give you some of your sister's medication?"

Momma was angry at Danny. Although she hit, kicked and screamed at him, he knew it was nothing compared to the fear of watching it happen to Louise.

Once Danny had all the glass cleaned up, Momma banished everyone to their rooms on that sunny Saturday afternoon. She turned on the radio in the kitchen, humming with, 'Sing a Song', by The Carpenters.

It was not the last time that Danny was to be the protector. Not by a long shot.

CHAPTER 11

PROVING GROUND

The first hint that Danny was supposed to be growing up came when he saw Momma loading the Cadillac when they got home from school one day. Both Mark and he looked at each other strangely as Momma loaded up bag after bag into the trunk of the car.

"What's going on?" Danny asked.

"How about helping me out?" Momma asked busily.

"With what?" Mark asked.

"Go to your room and get your toys, every last one of them. It's time that you learned how to be an adult. I expect the Lego set, Erector sets and every last toy car that you have up there. We're going to Goodwill and giving these to kids who can use them."

"But..." Danny started to say. It was akin to taking the last beer in the world from an alcoholic.

"But nothing! You get up to your room or are we going to have to discuss this with your father?"

There was no room for arguments when Momma threatened the wrath of Daddy. The two boys spent the next hour unloading the toy chest.

Louise was in her room, packing her Barbie doll sets, dollhouse and various other toys. All the kids silently did as they were told. If one were to watch them carefully, they would have seen tears slipping out of their eyes.

Mark and Danny put their Hot Wheels in a bag and hid them in the back of the closet, under some shoes. They could part with anything except for their cars. There was no way that Momma was getting hold of those. At the last second, Mark decided that they should keep a couple of cars separate from the bag. Namely, the pink and blue Lincoln Mark Ill's, the yellow and red Custom Corvettes, the purple and green Eldorado' and the olive green and tan Terero's were hidden under the mattress in case Momma found the stash in the closet.

Just before they left to Goodwill, Momma found the stash in the closet. It would be remembered as one of the most traumatic days of their lives.

An hour later, three sullen kids were back at home feeling that their lives were over. Their toys, like departed old friends, were gone forever. While Daddy was eating his dinner, the house was eerily quiet.

"What happened to your hand?" Daddy asked Momma while they were eating.

Danny was tip-toeing up the stairs by the kitchen when he stopped to listen.

Mark and Louise had been banished to their rooms, a common place to be ever since Momma had lost her temper with Louise recently.

"Nothing," Momma answered.

"It's obvious that something happened, with a bandage that big," Daddy pursued.

"A couple of days ago, I was washing dishes and I cut my hand. When we were on the way to Goodwill, the wound re-opened itself. That's it," Momma lied.

"Well, you don't have to get so sharp with me," Daddy said. "I've had a rough day, too, you know."

"I know, honey. You always have rough days. Can't I have one once in a while?"

The two of them ate in silence while Danny waited motionless and intently on the stairs.

"What's happening to us?" Momma asked.

"Huh?"

"I hit Louise the other day."

"What for?" Daddy asked.

"She clammed up. She wouldn't answer me when I asked her why she was roughhousing the living room. I just lost my temper..."

"Could you help it? These kids are getting more defiant and difficult every day," Daddy said. "We all lose our tempers every once in a while. My father did it all the time, but did it hurt me? Look at how I turned out. It's just discipline, that's all. One day, they'll be happy that we raised them in a strict environment. You have to remember that we're only doing the best for them."

"But, I still feel bad..." Momma said quietly.

"And didn't you feel bad when you had to smack Cookie for urinating on the floor when she was a kitten?"

"Yes, but..."

"It's all a part of being a parent. Next time, she'll think twice about roughhousing behind your back. I think you did the right thing. We have a lot of expensive things in there that we would be heartbroken to lose. If she wants to act carelessly, she can wait until she's outside. Otherwise, we will not put up with it in my house. Next time, she'll understand that."

Momma appeared to think about it for a moment. "Thanks, I feel a little better," she said.

"So, do you want to get Danny down here to talk about what we talked about last night?"

Upon hearing his name, he quickly dashed upstairs to the safe confines of his room. What was he in trouble for now, he thought.

"Danny?" Daddy called from downstairs.

"Yes?" Danny answered.

"Come down here. We'd like to talk to you."

"I'm coming," Danny called back as he ran down the stairs.

Danny walked to the doorway of the kitchen and stood with his hands behind his back. He tried not to be jealous of the stuffed pork chops and au gratin potatoes. Pangs of hunger gnawed at his stomach, even though he had just eaten an hour before. Momma had bragged about the dinner that she had served the kids, consisting of a plate of "No Brand" macaroni and cheese.

She had gotten four boxes for a dollar and learned that each box served four kids at a time. Not bad, for a quarter.

"What does trust mean to you?" Daddy asked, while stuffing a big piece of juicy pork into his mouth.

"Trust?" Danny asked, not knowing what he was referring to.

"Yes, trust. Give me the definition of trust. Are you deaf?"

"Well, no. Trust is when you believe in someone."

"That answer will work for the time being, I suppose." Daddy looked up from his plate, pointing his fork at Danny. It was loaded with creamy potatoes. "Can we trust you?"

"Well, yes," Danny said while wringing his hands behind his back. It looked like this might pan out to be a long quiz session. God only knew where it was headed.

"Why do you say that we can trust you?"

Danny nervously pondered the question for a moment. He hated these quiz sessions. They usually never amounted to anything but trouble for him. He fumbled for the proper words. "Because I'm trying to be a good son."

"Yes, you've been trying, haven't you?" Momma piped in sarcastically. "You've run away from home, you've lied, forged and God only knows that those are only the things we've caught you doing. Are you trying to call that someone to trust?"

"Well, no."

"Do you want to be trusted?"

"Yes."

"Why?" Daddy asked.

"Um, so I won't be a bad son," Danny answered, like he thought he was supposed to.

"Oh, great. I feel safe now," Daddy said, sarcasm dripping from his voice. He looked at Momma without saying anything, as if he was reconsidering.

Danny wrung and twisted his hands behind his back, consciously trying not to look at their dinner.

"Do you know why we took your toys away?" Momma asked.

"Because we've been bad and we can't be trusted?" Danny said as a question.

"No, Danny," Daddy said. "It's because you're now thirteen years-old and it's time that you faced responsibility. You've got no time for toys, anymore. We've decided that, as much as your mother has opposed this, we should begin to trust you. Do you think that that's a mistake?"

"No."

"I hope not because if we find out that this is a mistake, there's going to be a price to pay. Do you understand me?"

"Yes, Daddy," he answered, knowing very well what Daddy meant by saying, "a price to pay."

"We're going to start square dancing, again. Your father and I used to do it a long time ago, before we were burdened with having you. We think that it's time for us to start enjoying ourselves again. So, if we can trust you, we want you to babysit your brother and sister on Thursday night and every Thursday thereafter. Can you handle that?"

"Yes, Momma."

"We're going to be gone from six o'clock until eleven or twelve o'clock. There are some very strict rules to be followed and we want them followed to the letter. Do you understand?"

"Yes," Danny answered, already excited about this new prospect of freedom.

"Now, Danny," She enunciated clearly, "we've thought about this a lot and we have no choice. Our square dancing is going to be held at K.I. Sawyer Air Force Base in Gwinn. It's a long drive out there. We'd rather have sent you to Mrs. Thill's but it would make it too difficult for us. Besides, she charges a lot of money, money we could save by trusting you to babysit instead. So, the only viable solution that we can come up with is to trust you with the welfare of your brother and sister. I'll have you know that it's against our best intentions. Is that clear?"

"Yes," Danny answered, doing his best to keep his excitement at bay.

"If you let us down, you'll be the sorriest boy on the face of this earth. We're giving you only one chance. If you ever let us down, you'll never be trusted again. But, we have to start somewhere. Can you be trusted?"

"Yes," Danny answered again. He knew he was being trusted because of the money they would save rather than because it was an attempt at having a "normal" family.

"Good, champ," Daddy said. "We begin on a trial basis, tomorrow night."

The next night, he was trusted to babysit his siblings. Momma was not kidding when she said that there were going to be some strict rules.

Each child was placed in a separate room in the house with Mark in his bedroom, the door shut and locked and Louise was to stay in the basement, under the same conditions. Danny was assigned to stay in the kitchen where he could monitor any attempt at misbehaving. The situation was set up so that all the kids would be as far apart as possible thus alleviating any chance for shenanigans. Momma emphasized that it was a privilege for Danny to be allowed to stay up so late, since he normally was sent to bed by 8:30.

She also made it clear that not only was he to watch out for the welfare of his brother and sister, he was in charge of their two million dollar house.

Each rule was laid down, to be obeyed with an 'or else' clause. Mark and Louise were to be in bed by 8:00, or else. They were not allowed to have any contact; including not speaking with each other. Or else. They were not allowed to leave the rooms designated to them, or else.

"Are we clear?" Momma asked, after each rule was spelled out.

For the first few Thursdays, each rule was adhered to as laid out. None of the kids moved from their rooms and the house was just as quiet as it would have been if Momma and Daddy were there. The only thing noticeably different was the lack of tension when the parents were out of the house.

After a while, Danny modified the rules, somewhat. So what? He thought.

They weren't doing anything bad, they just acted like a little family. Danny would wait about an hour after Momma and Daddy left, in case they came right back after forgetting something, and, when he felt the risk was minimal for a premature return, he would let his brother and sister out of their respective rooms. At first, they were nervous as rabbits, trapped in a potential fox-hole. They would creep out of their rooms, unsure of what to do with their newly found freedom, like a fawn wandering from the safety of a mother deer.

A few Thursdays later, they found themselves getting comfortable with it, and looking forward to it. If one were to look in the windows unobserved, they would see the three kids sitting on the floor in the family room, watching re-runs of, 'The Three Stooges' and of, 'The Honeymooners', laughing every time that Ralph said, "To the moon, Alice!" Or, they might be seen playing Yahtzee or Chinese checkers. On another occasion, they might have been seen playing Frisbee or flying gliders outside.

The kids felt normal. It was great, being able to talk out loud, without disturbing their parents. If they felt like laughing with glee, no one would be any the wiser. There were no quizzes and they weren't called things like, "disobedient, lying, insolent brats."

And, a good hour before Momma and Daddy came home, Danny would make sure that each kid was returned to their respective rooms. They came to enjoy the brief, weekly respite from their parents' ruling hand. Danny always made sure to rush them off to their rooms with the admonishment that they must never tell Momma or Daddy, an admonishment reiterated the night they played 'Doctor', an activity that surely would have resulted in the belt should they have been discovered.

During those Thursdays, the kids became closer to each other. Thursdays gave them a break and something to look forward to. Regardless of what was happening on any given day, they always knew that they had Thursdays to look forward to. Thursday was a day of magical escape for them and it never came soon enough and when it did, it passed too quickly.

The one thing that helped Danny cope was his old friend, Robbie Feshter. They had been inseparable best friends ever since they had moved back from Detroit. Danny had known him since kindergarten, almost as long his brother. Momma and Daddy didn't like him too much saying that he was a typical Yooper because of an impression Robbie had made on Daddy, back when he was seven or eight years-old.

"Hi, I'm Robbie." He was introduced while Daddy was mowing the lawn one summer day.

"Well, hello," Daddy answered in a friendly enough tone of voice. "Aren't you the boy that I met sledding down my driveway late one night?"

Robbie blushed and extended his hand. "It's good to meet you, Mr. Wilcox."

"Dr. Wilcox," Daddy corrected. He went back to mowing the lawn, leaving Robbie standing there, his hand still extended.

Since then, Robbie was labeled a "hick" and a bad influence on Danny.

Daddy figured that Robbie was just another Yooper who was ignorant of how hard Daddy worked for that town. It was just as well. Robbie didn't like Daddy much, either. He was polite enough not to let him know.

With the exception of his brother, Robbie and Danny were as close as two boys could get. Whenever they had the chance, they would do everything together. They looked at their first Playboy together. Once, they were stung a hundred times each, during an impromptu apple fight they had had in Farmer's Field. They got lost in the woods on countless numbers of adventures while they killed each other a thousand times while play fighting, imitating G.I. Joe. During the winter, they went sledding until their boots were packed with twenty pounds of ice.

One day, they snow skitched the bus, and it was the first of many secrets that they ended up sharing. It was about six-thirty in the morning when they met at the bus stop. Both of them were buried in thick parkas. Before the bus pulled up, they both hid in the bushes, undetected, waiting for its arrival. When the other kids piled on, Baldy, the bus driver, pulled the door closed. Danny and Robbie scooted to the rear bumper. As Baldy pressed the accelerator, each boy made sure that they had a firm hold as they got in a slouched over position and waited for the ride of their lives. As he drove to the next stop, the two boys could be seen laughing as they were sliding on their heels behind it. Skitching the bus was an adventure in and of itself, better than the traveling carnival that came every spring. They usually got coated with packed snow from the rear wheels but it was a thrill that only kids could understand. They went through three stops and decided to gamble on one more stretch when lightning struck.

The city had salted the roads, unbeknownst to the boys, about an hour before. To the dismay of the adventurous friends, there was a section of the road where the salt had melted the snow, leaving a stretch of bare and wet asphalt. The boys found out quickly that bare pavement is not conducive to skitching a bus properly as they went sprawling, face first, dragging behind the bus. The next thing they knew, they were tumbling head over heels, trying to remember their prayers from catechism. The bus pulled to a screaming halt when the passengers alerted Baldy. He jumped out of the bus and came running up to them.

"Jesus, kids! You okay?" he asked worriedly.

"I think so," Robbie and Danny answered in unison.

"Goddammit! You scared the bejesus out of me!"

"We're sorry, Baldy," Danny said, his head down, ashamed at being caught.

Suddenly, Baldy started laughing. "No harm done. I can't rightly say that I'm going to be upset 'cause it ain't the first time it's happened. I used to do the same thing. Next time, though, don't do it with me driving, eh? I'm getting too old to be picking up body parts on the street."

"You're not going to tell our parents, are you?" asked Danny.

"Ya never know, eh?" Baldy said with a wink.

"How come you always wear make-up?" Robbie asked Danny one day while they were fishing under the old Harvey bridge.

Danny was taken aback for a moment. He was embarrassed. "My mom makes us wear it."

"That's the weirdest thing I ever heard," Robbie commented.

"Look at this," Danny said as he bunched up his pant leg up to his knee.

Robbie looked at the scars on Danny's shins. "What are those from?"

"My dad's wing-tipped shoes did that. He kicks us all the time. Look under my arms."

Danny pushed his shirt sleeve up as far as it would go so that he could show his friend the underside of his biceps. Small scabs detailed cuts in arm. "It's from my mom squeezing our arms. Her fingernails cut into the skin."

"That's mean," Robbie said.

"It hurts, too. My mom puts make-up on so that nobody will see the damage."

"Is that why you never go to gym class?"

"We never go to gym after getting the belt," Danny answered. "My dad writes us doctor notes and won't let us back to class until the bruising heals."

"That's not normal," Robbie commented. "You should go to the police."

"The police would never believe us."

"I don't remember your parents doing that the last time you lived up here."

Danny cast his line back in the water. "It wasn't so bad. It didn't get bad until we moved to Detroit. I think it is because my family ran out of money and they got stressed out. When we came back to Marquette, it got worse instead of going away."

"All the kids at school think you guys are weird and nobody likes your parents. I think if they knew what was happening to you, they might feel different."

"I don't think anyone cares," Danny said quietly.

"I've got an idea," Robbie said casually as he recast his line into the water. They rarely caught any fish but it was fun to hope. The animals made their noises in the woods and insects appeared to play tag on the water while an occasional train would shake their worlds, overhead.

The only time that they had ever caught a fish down there was the first time that they had been there. Somehow, Robbie managed to keep from getting hauled into the water when he snared what surely seemed as big as a shark. As it turned out, it was not a shark but rather a pregnant Rainbow Trout, its multi-colored scales gleaming in the sun. Robbie wanted to keep it but Danny suggested that they throw it back in the water.

"Imagine all the trout that'll be in this stream when all those eggs hatch," Danny prodded.

Robbie agreed and that had become their fishing spot from then on.

"So, what's your idea?" Danny asked while he watched his worm squirm in the abnormally frigid waters.

"About your parents," Robbie stated. "Why don't you tell someone else in your family? You have grandparents, aunts and uncles, don't you?"

"They all live in Detroit," Danny responded.

"All grandparents care about children. Why not call you your Dad's mom or your Mom's mom? I bet they would listen."

Danny tugged on his line absentmindedly. "I don't think it would help the situation. I haven't talked my grandma on my Dad's side in years. She used to write me letters all the time but Dad got mad at her."

"What about your other grandma?" Robbie asked.

"There's no way she would believe me. She likes my mother too much."

Robbie reeled his line in. "You need to do something."

"No, Danny, listen. I've been thinking about it and I think it could work if you did it right."

"Robbie, please?" Danny pleaded, testily. It was too nice a day to jump into a conversation about his parents.

Robbie casually cast his line a little further upstream. "Really. Listen to this plan."

"Okay, I'll listen. But, don't expect me to follow through on it. If it's stupid, I'm going to tell you, alright? So, don't get pissed off at me."

"I won't," Robbie said. "Record them."

"What?"

"My dad has a tape recorder. We could tape them when they're slapping you guys around."

"We?" Danny questioned. "You mean me." He watched his feet as they dangled in the water and chewed on it. "It'll never work. How am I supposed to do that? Wait for my dad to start beating the crap out of Mark and then run and grab the tape recorder and stand there while he does it?"

"Sort of."

"Forget it," Danny said dejectedly.

"Seriously, Danny. Let's just say that they start picking on Mark. You've got the tape recorder hidden in your bed or something. If Mark is getting beaten up or something, shove the tape recorder in your shirt and sneak to someplace nearby. All you have to do is hit the 'record' button."

"Oh, sure, Robbie. And what happens if I get caught?"

"No guts, no glory."

"Fine, so I record them. What do I do with the tape?"

Robbie tugged on his line a bit. "Don't be dumb. You take the tape to the police station and make them listen to it. They'll hear it and they'll have proof that something's wrong. You'll go to court or something and then you can live with me and my parents."

When Robbie put it that way, it was too tempting for Danny to ignore. He reluctantly agreed to Robbie's plan.

Days later, Robbie took the tape recorder without telling his parents and gave it to Danny, complete with a fresh tape and new batteries. Robbie said that his parents would not notice its disappearance.

Danny hid it in the garage, behind Daddy's boat. A day or so later, he managed to sneak it upstairs to his bedroom and hide it between the support slats underneath his bed.

It was a matter of waiting it out for the perfect scenario.

Unfortunately, for the longest time, whenever Daddy would get mad with the kids, Danny was nowhere near the tape recorder. Even if it was within reach, he was too afraid to use it. The tape recorder remained hidden, untouched.

To the disadvantage of Louise, there came an evening when Daddy began his usual fare with her while helping with her studies. Danny had been in his room doing his studies when he became distracted by her growing screams. At the very moment that it pissed him off, he thought of the hidden recorder. For a moment, he froze. He didn't think he could do it. He heard the sound of her getting smacked followed by a yelp as Daddy began pulling her hair. Something inside Danny snapped, and he reached under the bed for the tape recorder. He felt the cool plastic of the machine and carefully slipped it out. His hands were shaking as he crept over to his bedroom doorway. In the kitchen, Louise's screaming intensified.

Danny looked down the hallway, both ways. Seeing no one, he stuck the recorder out, so that it faced in the direction of the kitchen. He did not dare creep down the stairs as it was far too risky. He pressed the 'record' button, thinking, "Scream your heart out, Louise. It'll be the last time. Scream as loudly as you can."

Danny heard the kitchen stool fall back against the kitchen table, as it usually did when Daddy lost his patience. Daddy hit and Louise screamed. The tape recorder was running all the while. Before the recorder stopped, Danny turned it off and hid it back under the bed.

When he went to sleep that night, he felt strong and victorious.

Although easier said than done, Danny managed to sneak the tape recorder out of the house early the next morning. Once he rounded the bend of the driveway, the recorder hidden in his shirt, he ran all the way to Robbie's house. He kept it hidden when he knocked on Robbie's door, so that his parents wouldn't see it. If they had seen it, he knew that Robbie would get into trouble and there was enough trouble going around without getting someone else involved.

"Oh, hi," Robbie said through the screen door.

"I got it!" Danny said excitedly, in a loud whisper.

"Got what?"

"I taped my dad last night!"

"No kidding?" Robbie said, disbelievingly. "Mom? I'll be right back. I'm going outside and play with Danny for a little while."

"Don't go too far away," she hollered from somewhere in the house.

"Lunch will be ready soon. Danny? Would you like some lunch?"

"No, thank you, Mrs. Feshter," he answered. "I'm not allowed."

"Oh, Danny. You know you're always welcome here."

"I already ate," Danny lied. He didn't trust adults very much, even if it was Robbie's mom. She'd probably accidentally tell his parents and then he'd get his butt kicked for 'free-loading'.

"Have it your way," she answered with what sounded like a smile. She was like what a real mom should be.

The two kids took off into the woods behind Robbie's house.

"Well, are you going to play it or what?" Robbie asked when they found a suitable place beneath an aged Birch tree.

Danny hit the 'play' button and heard nothing.

"Did you rewind it?" Robbie asked.

"Oops," Danny said, realizing what was wrong. He rewound it. Both boys listened intently when he hit the 'play' button again. They heard the squeal of the leader and then the hiss of the tape as it began. Danny's palms were sweaty with anticipation. This would be the moment of truth. He finally had obtained proof. They sat upright and raised the volume of the player.

"Mmmmf mmm...mf...mf...mmmf," it said, muffled.

A look of disbelief crossed Danny's face.

"I didn't hear what it said," Robbie commented.

Danny rewound it and tried it again.

"Mmmmf mmm...mf...mf...mmmf," the tape repeated.

Danny felt like he was going to cry in frustration, but couldn't in front of his best friend. He looked at Robbie. Robbie looked back, comprehending their failure.

"Shoot! I knew it wouldn't work," Danny said, forcefully holding back his tears. "It didn't tape good at all!"

"We'll try it again, okay?" Robbie offered supportively. "Don't worry. There'll be other times. Next time, just get closer when they do it! We'll get it right, okay? We aren't going to give up just like that!"

"Yeah, maybe next time," Danny said, dejectedly. "If we live that long."

CHAPTER 12

CRY FOR HELP

For months, Danny and Robbie tried to conceive ways of how they could finally nail Momma and Daddy. Once, because Danny said that his father was in a bad mood, Robbie stood under one of the eaves of the house in the backyard, tape recorder in hand. It was Robbie's idea to hide out back there. He figured that he could be a witness in court, in the event that something happened. Robbie's hiding turned out to be to no avail. Since it had been drizzling all day long, the only thing that Robbie got out of it was a whopper of a cold. It was just Danny's luck. Just when he wanted something to happen, nothing did. His parents were too damned unpredictable.

Although Danny told Robbie a hundred times how much he appreciated his trying to help, Danny knew that Robbie would eventually begin to doubt his word. Before something really bad happened, Danny felt that he had to prove his case to someone. To Danny's discouragement, something always got in the way. Either Danny was not close enough to the incident when it happened, whereby the taping of it proved useless, or the incident was too minor for the taping of it to be worthwhile.

It frustrated Danny to no end. His father's reputation was no help, either

Who would believe that a doctor, one who provided such a service to the town, was also the same man who beat his children? Was child abuse occurring on "Doctor's Row" in Shiras Hills, the affluent neighborhood of the city? Who would take a child's word over an adult's, unless Danny could prove it?

Danny also worried over the increase of the incidences. It seemed like it was happening all of the time, never when he could prove it, and each incident was getting a little more ferocious than the incident prior. He worried so much that he couldn't sleep with the intrusion of terribly vivid nightmares.

Something inside was telling him that something really bad was about to happen. It was inevitable. All it would take is one time where just a fraction of strength was just a little too much, like the straw that broke the camel's back. If that happened, Danny thought, he would surely never be able to live with himself. He would feel responsible because he was sure that there was a way he could stop it. But how would he do it? If he worked just a little harder, the inevitable might be averted. Danny thought that somebody could die, somebody who was frail and defenseless, like Louise. He wished, a thousand times, that he could walk into the police station and get it over with. But, if the police didn't believe him, he would surely be sent back home to face a father who would most certainly take it out on his hide. If he thought that missing school for a couple of weeks was bad, imagine what would happen when he came back from trying to turn his father in to the police.

Everything was going to hell in a bucket and he was powerless to stop it.

Summer merged into fall and fall blew into winter, always returning much faster than anyone wanted. The thing about winter in the Upper Peninsula was that it was about seven months too long with temperatures that would freeze an ear in a minute and bring pain to your fingers. It kept people in the house, for months at a time, waiting anxiously for the first spring thaw, which was always too far away. When Stephen King published, 'The Shining', people in Northern Michigan understood cabin fever. Cabin fever, in a house like that of the Wilcox's, could be life-threatening, no question about it.

It was in the middle of one of the coldest February's on record, with temperatures plummeting to well below zero, that Daddy got a call from Marquette General Hospital for an emergency. They needed him right away, as a man had just attempted to drink a bottle of Drano, in a failed suicide attempt. As Daddy had said, the liquid never made it down the man's throat. The acid reduced the man's tongue and jaw to nothing more than dangling flesh. Daddy had to go to the hospital to attempt some sort of reconstruction, something he apparently did not relish at the time. It was too damn cold out to go anywhere. Daddy knew that it would be a time-consuming effort, probably taking him the better part of the night. Momma had hoped for a quiet evening with him and, again, she would be deprived.

Danny made a mental note never to attempt suicide via the Drano method. It sounded gruesome and, most importantly, it didn't work.

As soon as Daddy left, the tension in the house dissipated. It was always worse when both parents were home. When only one parent was home, it seemed that the chances of getting smacked were greatly reduced. The only other time that the children did not feel the overbearing nervousness and tension, was when Daddy was sick in bed with the flu, a common occurrence during those frigid winters. The kids were quiet while he was in bed recovering, but that meant that Momma also had to be quiet. She would not dare hit the kids while Daddy was sleeping for fear that they would wake him up. Daddy was not in a good mood if he was awakened prematurely, as everyone was well aware.

It was strange, the way Momma was changing. One could never predict her moods. One day she would be great, the next, she would be down and the kids would suffer for it. On that particularly frigid Friday night, an icy wind blew, driving temperatures down twenty degrees below zero, which magnified an already touchy situation.

Cabin fever had drawn itself to a fever pitch.

Danny was in the study downstairs, looking through Daddy's library for a book to read. He had finished his nightly chores while Mark and Louise were still working on theirs. Louise was supposed to be cleaning the bathroom, adjacent to the study, while Mark was supposed to be cleaning the laundry room, next to the bathroom. Instead, Danny could hear Mark and Louise playing "tag" in hushed tones in the laundry room. Danny listened with amusement while they played, thinking that it sounded like fun, but not daring to get involved. Like his brother and sister, he had let his guard down for a moment.

"You're it!" he heard Mark whisper excitedly.

"No, I'm not! You didn't touch me!"

"I did, too!"

"No, you didn't!" Louise corrected, playfully. "It's still your turn to get me!"

The sound of pattering feet followed, as they chased each other around the laundry room. Danny could hear that each one was running out of breath. Every once in a while, he heard an occasional giggle.

"I gotcha!" Mark said, the sound of victory in his voice.

The sound of a crash followed, as one of them fell into the laundry room closet doors. The noise seemed to reverberate down the hallway. Obviously, someone had been attempting to avoid a tag and had miscalculated their step. Danny froze, as did the occupants of the laundry room. They all waited in silent panic for Momma to come rushing downstairs, demanding to know what the noise had been.

Silence permeated the air for one infinitesimal minute.

"We better stop," Danny heard Mark whisper to Louise. "Let's get back to doing our duties before we get into trouble."

"Okay," Louise said. "But you're still it!"

"Am not!"

"Are so"

"Am not!" Mark whispered back.

Danny was just pulling a book off of a shelf, when he saw Momma's shadow go fleeting by in the direction of the laundry room. His stomach lurched.

"What the hell is going on here?" Momma asked, breaking the silence.

"Nothing!" Mark answered defensively. Danny knew that he must have just about dumped in his drawers with Momma's unexpected appearance. He could hear it in his voice.

"Then what was that big crash that I just heard?!"

"I don't know!" Louise answered in a guilt-ridden voice.

"That's right, Momma," Mark defended. "I don't know what you heard, either!"

Danny crept over to one side of the den where he could observe the developing situation, undetected, by looking into the hallway mirror which gave him clear sight to the laundry room. It was at a moment like that that he wished that he had the tape recorder within easy access. But, it was all the way upstairs and he didn't think that Momma knew that he was in the den. He hoped that it wouldn't be one of those times.

"And what are you two doing in here together, when I specifically separated you by putting you in the bathroom and you in the laundry room?"

Momma demanded to know.

Mark tried to exit the situation by saying, "I'm sorry, we'll finish right now!"

"Oh, no you won't. Not until I have an answer out of you! What happened here?"

"I don't know," Louise repeated, her voice level rising to a light screech.

Danny watched Momma walk over to Louise and grab her under the arm.

He was very aware of the pain that Louise was feeling as Momma dug her fingernails into the tender flesh under her arms. Louise winced in pain, squirming to get away.

"You nincompoop! I want an answer out of you and don't you dare say, 'I don't know'."

"Oww...it hurts...please, Momma, don't!"

"You disobedient little retard!" Momma shouted at her, shaking the daylights out of her. With her other hand, she started slapping Louise in the face. "Fine! Don't answer! I'll keep doing this until you do!"

"Cut it out, Momma!" Mark suddenly yelled.

Momma let Louise go and looked at Mark, her face turning red. "Well, I'll be," she said. "Have we got a tough boy here?"

"No," Mark answered, his courage greatly diminished. He had a look on his face that said he had just realized what a grave mistake he had made.

Momma placed her hands on her hips and looked at him, as if she was trying to determine what form of punishment best suited his crime.

Danny watched the rest happen, as if it was in slow motion. Disbelief painted his trembling features, like a slowly advancing shadow. He shouldn't have been shocked at the sight; it was practically status quo, except for Thursday nights. It was to be expected, ignored and forgotten.

Momma's hands suddenly reached out, one grabbing Louise's head and the other, grabbing Mark's. She brought both heads together, which created a resounding crack. They both answered in simultaneous cries of pain.

Danny, the onlooker, was biting his lip in a fit of anger and frustration, unaware of the blood dripping down his chin. Bitter tears flooded his eyes as he watched, while his brother and sister stood there in a sobbing daze, when his mother lost her mind like he had never quite seen before. Her feet started kicking them repeatedly while her clenched fists flailed over their heads.

An overpowering sense of anger blossomed in Danny with every second increasing its intensity. His role as the protector resurfaced: he had to stop it! The first thought was that he could run in there and overpower her. He quickly dismissed that in watching how angry she was, though. She was too angry and she would surely kill him. What she was doing to Mark presently, because of his attempt to stop it, was convincing enough. He thought of the tape recorder, but that was upstairs. There was no way that he could get out of the study without her seeing him. Once again, he felt like his hands were tied behind his back.

The wind howled outside, causing the windows to rattle.

As he watched in eye-widening horror, Momma grabbed the mop that Mark had been using to clean the floor. She raised it above her head and cracked the handle down on the helpless children. Danny wanted to scream but fear constricted his throat. He grabbed the hair at his temples and began pulling as hard as he could. His eyes were squeezed shut, oblivious of his own pain, as he tried to block out the sounds of their echoing screams. As the screams increased in intensity, Momma seemed to increase the frequency of blows with the mop handle.

Danny turned around toward the desk. The telephone sat there, its black surface reflecting the glow of the incandescent lights. He had to do it now! Danny found the drive to dash over to the desk, making sure that his movement wasn't seen. He picked up the receiver and dialed the number to the police department as fast as he could. It took him three times to dial the number because of his trembling fingers. His tears also made it hard for him to read the sticker on the base of the telephone, which had a listing of all the emergency numbers. The sticker had been placed on all of the telephones in the house when Danny had started babysitting. Danny never realized what he would really use that number for.

"Hello?" he said in hushed whisper, his hand cupped over the mouthpiece.

"Yes, This is the Marquette County Police Department," a lady's flat and disinterested voice repeated.

"I have to report something right away," Danny said quickly. His brother and sister were still screaming in the background, telling him that he was safe from Momma's attention for the moment. As long as she was hitting, he still had time. He kept glancing toward the mirror in the hallway but the angle prevented him from seeing what was happening in the laundry room. He didn't have much time.

"How can we help you?"

"My mother is beating my brother and sister to death!" Danny said urgently. "You have to help us!"

"If this is some kind of joke," she said, irritated.

"It's not! Listen!" Danny said. He held the phone in the direction of the echoing screams for about thirty seconds, time enough for the person on the other end of the line to understand what was happening. "Did you hear that?" he asked.

"I couldn't hear anything," she answered, obviously unshaken.

"What do you mean you couldn't hear anything?" Danny asked in exasperation. "Please! I'm serious! She's going to kill one of them any second now!"

"Let me speak to one of your parents, son," the operator demanded.

"You don't understand..." Danny said, stopping. He hung up the phone, knowing that there was no point in continuing the phone call. Damn it, he thought, why won't anyone believe me? He heard the sound of a crash as somebody fell into one of the closet doors. He crept over to where he could see what was happening in the mirror.

Momma was repeatedly slamming Mark's head into the closet door.

It was then that Danny saw a sight that he would never see again. Louise reached out to Momma's back. Although she did it very hesitantly, she did it.

Danny knew exactly what Louise was doing in that simple gesture. She was reaching out to plead with Momma to stop it.

Danny could read it on her red and tear-stained face. Within that moment, Louise looked incredibly small in size compared to her mother but her courage made up for it. She paused a moment then, slowly, reached over and tugged on the back of Momma's blouse.

Momma turned around and glared. It was as if Momma knew the exact intentions that Louise had at that moment, and couldn't believe that Louise could be stupid enough to show such belligerence and gall. She went to slap her, but Louise quickly raised her arm up to defend herself, almost knowing Momma would react in exactly that way. Momma's hand collided with her arm.

"You little creep! You hurt me!" Momma screamed at her. Momma turned around to grab anything she could. Danny saw that the mop was a discarded weapon, lying on the floor, the handle broken in half. On the washing machine, Momma's hand found an aerosol can of Spray 'N Wash.

Using the can like a club, she brought it down upon Louise's head. A popping sound followed.

Blood suddenly showered the flowered, wall-papered walls. It squirted straight up from Louise's head, bringing the room to silence as droplets hit the door and sprayed Momma in their ferocity.

Danny was watching it all, frozen in shock.

Louise's knees collapsed, bringing her to the floor. The spray can dropped out of Momma's hand, as she stood there, watching the blood spray, maybe wondering if she had just killed her daughter. Maybe realizing that, this time, she had gone too far.

"Danny!" Momma screeched. "Get down here!"

"Yes, Momma," Danny answered after a few moments. He quickly wiped the drying blood off of his own chin and ran into the laundry room.

"Start cleaning up this blood!" she ordered him. "We have to get Louise to the hospital." She grabbed a towel and wrapped it around Louise's head.

Louise's face was becoming pale and lucid, with a lack of any emotion except what appeared to be shock.

"See! This is what you two get for not doing what you're told to do! If you hadn't have been roughhousing, this would never have happened. You remember whose fault this is!" she reminded them. "Mark! Take a good look at what you've done to your sister. I hope you're happy!"

"I'm sorry, Momma," Mark replied with a confused look.

"Damn it!" Momma said to no one in particular. "When we get to the hospital, after Danny finishes cleaning up this mess, I had better hear all of you telling the doctor that this happened while you were playing. Do you understand me?!"

"Yes, Momma," Danny and Mark answered simultaneously.

Danny cleaned up as fast as he could, all the while, scared for the life of his sister. What if she died while he was still cleaning? He was angry at the police, too. If they had listened instead of jerking him around, this never would have happened, he thought frantically. Danny stood up when he finished wiping the blood up, dropping the rags in the laundry room sink.

"Don't forget to wipe it off the door!" Momma ordered him. "I don't want your father knowing about this!"

Danny did as he was told. Once the cleaning passed inspection, Momma and the children got into the car and drove silently to the hospital. She made sure that they didn't go to Marquette General Hospital, where Daddy was working, but rather to Holy Cross Hospital, an extra fifteen minutes away. On the way over, the only sounds that could be heard were the weeping and groaning noises made by Louise, as she held the towel to her head. Danny watched her white blouse darken with the growing stain of blood. Danny and Mark looked at each other, communicating their sentiments without opening their mouths. The same question was conveyed in each other's eyes: Was Louise going to die?

As soon as they arrived at the emergency room, Momma walked Louise in while Danny and Mark followed silently. Momma spoke to a doctor, after she explained who her husband was. Danny listened to the lies that poured out of Momma's mouth.

"Oh, you know kids," she said nervously. "They're always getting into some sort of mischief. Look what happened. Her brother, evidently, took a thong and smacked Louise with it.   I can't tell you how many times that I've told them to stop hitting each other but they just won't listen," she explained quickly. "It's not bad, is it? I love her so much! She'll be okay, won't she?"

Momma spoke like a completely different person, especially compared to the one she had been an hour prior. She assumed a persona likened to that of their babysitter, Mrs. Thill, only the kids knew better. Although it made Danny and Mark angry, their primary concern was over whether Louise was going to live or die. It was not the time to deal with the truth. At least that's how Danny rationalized it. He didn't have the guts to tell the doctor the real truth. Sadly enough, he saw that the doctor appeared to have believed his mother's lies. Momma even went so far as to look like she was going to cry over Louise's fate.

The doctor went off with Louise, sending the rest of the family to the waiting room. Momma spoke only once, looking at Mark with a vengeance in her eyes, "I hope you're happy with what you did to your sister. See how disobedience pays?!"

Mark's eyes dropped to his lap, feeling responsible for everything that had happened.

Danny clenched his fists silently in hate and anger, while his tongue played with the delicate area inside his lip. It was from that point on, after reliving the memory of what he had seen in laundry room, that he decided that he hated his mother. Everything that had been taught to him of God and religion was all garbage. How could God allow something like that happen to his sister? How could God make the police ignore him? If there really was a God, Danny thought angrily, he would kill Momma for what she had done!

As it turned out, an hour and a half later, Louise received twenty-two stitches in her head. The doctor had said that it had been one of those freak things, her head getting cut where it had. The contact point had been directly over a blood vessel, which explained the profuse amount of blood. Again, it crossed Danny's mind to blurt the truth out to the doctor, but he kept his mouth shut knowing that it would have been an exercise in futility. If he was ever going to say anything, it had to be said when he knew that he wasn't going to be sent back to his parents. Little did he know that an opportunity to do that was closer than he could have imagined. For the moment, he had chickened out again, and that made him feel like a spineless piece of trash.

The return drive home was completed in silence as Sammy Davis, Jr. sang 'Candy Man' on the radio. Louise had a gauze bandage wrapped around her head and face, making her look like a mummy in a scary Saturday night movie. The doctor had told Momma to keep her head bandaged for the better part of a week, not wanting to risk the re-opening of the wound.

As soon as they got home, Momma sent Danny and Mark to bed. Just before sending Louise to bed, she looked at her.

"That looks ridiculous," she said in reference to the bandages. "We are not having the town asking questions about this. It looks like I beat you up all of the time. Well, you'll be fine. There's no need to keep these bandages on."

She removed the white bandages. "You had better not say a word about this to anyone, including your father," she warned.

"I won't, Momma," Louise answered obediently.

While Danny and Mark were in bed, silence settling over the house, they waited a long while before whispering. The bare branches of a tree scraped against the window in the winter wind.

"Danny?"

"Yeah?"

"It's gotta stop."

"I know."

Neither one of them had anything left to say that night. Each had cried silently, remembering the confused and dazed look that had been on Louise's face when they had been driving back in the car. The only thing that could have been seen on her face, through the bandages, were her eyes, distant and sad, which seemed to ask, "What happened? I didn't mean to do anything wrong. I'm sorry."

Yes, Danny thought, it has to stop, but how?

CHAPTER 13

PUSH COMES TO SHOVE

It was inevitable that somebody would throw a rock at the glass house that the Wilcox family lived in and it was only right that Danny be the one to shatter it.

After the incident with Louise and her going to the hospital, Danny felt like they were all walking on a very tight high wire. A thin line of reality was keeping him in his crumbling home.

Danny hoped that his parents would learn from their mistakes, but they didn't. As the mistakes were made, Danny, Mark and Louise could feel their time running out, with Thursdays as their only respite from hell.

Louise showed the worst signs of wear by withdrawing into a shell that no one could seem to penetrate, including her siblings. She hid in the dark territory of her mind, scared to move without having some sort of repercussions from Momma and Daddy. Her grades in school slipped with silence as her only armor of protection. If she did talk, it was only prompted by the continual ritual of quiz sessions from Momma and Daddy, ending in the same results. If she gave them an answer, it was always the wrong answer and she paid for it. It was not uncommon to see Momma operating on her bruises with a dab of make-up for school, the admonition clear: "If you say a word about this to anyone..."

Louise did not say a word about anything to anyone. She was a becoming a recluse who believed she was retarded, making her an easy target for childhood schoolmates. She was not loved by Momma, who said she wanted to give up on her while Daddy had become sour and bitter, believing that he was undeserving of such a defective daughter. They did not have to tell Louise that. She felt it every time that she was banished to her room.

Mark wasn't spared from the tiring effects of their environment, either. At times, an air of defiance showed, as if he was prompting Momma and Daddy to continue their charade. There was many a time that he could be seen whipping his lunchbox, in frustration, across the street, only to have to face Momma and explain why his Thermos was broken, again.

Spring was melting into summer, the period that none of the kids relished for they did not have the salvation of being at school five days a week.

Summer was a tirade of dealing with Momma and Daddy on a twenty-four hour basis, seven days a week. The pressure would build until one of them, in a cesspool of hate and fear, would snap. Mark finally ran away after Momma tirelessly whipped him with an evergreen branch. He couldn't take it. He just ran with only the clothes on his back. What surprised Danny was that Momma didn't even act phased by it.

She called Danny downstairs. "Do you see what you've done?" she asked calmly.

"No, Momma," Danny responded.

"You're the one who made Mark run away. I would suggest that you get him back here as soon as possible or you'll have to deal with your father when he gets home. You wouldn't want that would you?"

"Mark ran away?"

"Yes, Mark ran away. He thinks he can do that because of the example that you've set in this household."

"I didn't make him run away," Danny answered, keeping his defiance at bay. His dark side was threatening to surge.

"Don't you talk back to me, young man," Momma warned. "You're going to have something to run away for if you don't get him back here, pronto! Are you going to go get him, or are we going to wait until your father gets home and see what he thinks?!"

Danny left, obediently, his head hung in shame.

Danny pretty much knew where Mark was and why he had bolted, but he did not relish the thought of bringing his brother back. Heck, he wasn't too pleased himself about living at home. For the moment, though, he knew that he was stuck with this shitty duty. For him to be blamed for his brother running away, made it all that much more worse. On the way, he stopped at a local convenience store, King's Korner, and shoplifted a couple of Swingin' Wing Hot Wheels, a sort of barter gift. After that, he made his way to the infamous St. Peter's Cathedral.

As he walked up the steps leading to the huge oak doors, he couldn't help remembering the distasteful experience he had had there, on a rainy night a long time ago. Sure enough, he saw Mark's shadow in one of the pews.

"Hi, Mark. What's going on?" he asked as he slid into the pew next to him. He didn't bother to genuflect; after all, it was only a building; whose meaning was lost a long time ago.

"How did you find me?" Mark asked, none too pleased at seeing his brother so quickly.

"You told me that this is where you'd go if you ever ran away."

"Me and my big mouth," Mark said sullenly.

"Hey, I got you something," Danny said. He pulled out one of the Hot Wheels toys. "Here."

Mark's eyes lit up for a second. He ripped open the package, rolling the car on his hands. "Cool."

Danny followed suit with the other car. "I got one for me, too. Compliments of King's Korner."

They sat in silence for a moment.

"Go away, Danny."

"I can't, Mark. I'm your brother."

"Not anymore," Mark said. "I'm not going back." His voice sounded ghostly as it echoed off the walls of the ancient Cathedral.

"You gotta come home" Danny said, something he didn't want to say.

"I'm not going home. Ever!"

"Mark, please listen to me."

"I can't take it anymore, Danny. They're too mean to us. I'm scared all of the time. You're not supposed to be scared of your parents. You're not supposed to beg for food from other kids. It isn't right! They hit, scream and yell so much, it's like everything's out of control and they can't see it. It wasn't always like this," Mark said. He thought about it for a moment. "And how do you explain what happened to Louise?"

Danny could not say anything because he knew that his brother was right. He was torn by what he was supposed to do and what he wanted to do. Heck, he wanted to run away himself but it wasn't the right time. On the other side of the coin, there stood images of what his father would do if he did not return Mark to where he belonged.

"It was an accident," Danny said as convincingly as he could.

"Yeah, right," Mark returned scornfully. "And what about next time? Will it be an accident if they kill one of us? I just want to be normal, like other kids. This isn't fair and you know it!"

"I know it isn't fair, but we have to stick it out."

"I don't want to," Mark said. He proceeded to start bawling, oblivious of the echo chamber that they were in.

Danny put his arm around his little brother's shoulder, allowing him to let out some of the pain and frustration. He looked at the immense crucifix hanging over the altar, the blood dripping from the various wounds, and wondered if Christ's pain was anything like theirs.

Danny looked at his watch, figuring that they had an hour before Daddy got home. They didn't have much time. "We have to go back," he said quietly.

"Please don't take me back," Mark begged. "If you were any kind of big brother, you wouldn't do that."

He felt like he had been stabbed by his brother's stinging words, but he pushed. "Mark, listen to me. I have to take you back. I promise that I'll get you guys out of there, I just can't do it right now."

"You promise?"

"I promise but we have to tough it out just a little while longer."

Mark appeared to ponder the pros and cons of the situation. "Am I going to get the belt for this?"

"No, Mark. I promise that you won't get the belt."

"Well, okay," Mark said with a hint of relief. "You're a great brother, probably the best that one could have."

"Thanks, Mark."

"And thanks for the Swingin' Wing. I don't know what we'd do if it weren't for you and I and our Hot Wheels. I wish we had our other collection back, the ones that Momma gave away."

Mark and Danny took their time walking home, trying not to think about the parents that they didn't like, anymore.

Danny tried not thinking about the promises that he had made to his brother, promises that he was not sure he could follow through on. He felt like he had tricked his brother into coming home.

When Mark got the belt that night, Danny felt each blow ten times over. For every crack that Mark received, Danny was upstairs, hitting himself as hard as he could.

Push came to shove, not too long afterwards. The bits and pieces that Danny was not around for, he pieced together from Mark many months later. Danny's wish was going to come through, much sooner than he expected. He would be handed a silver platter with the opportunity to get the kids out of there. It all began with a conversation that Momma had with Louise.

It was a hot mid-August day, the type of day where the heat caused tempers to flare at the littlest of things. Momma was testy, in part because Daddy had been working a lot, leaving her with the responsibility of watching the kids, a chore that she was tiring of. Danny had been in the garage, going through his meager collection of glider parts in the toy box, hidden away so that Momma couldn't find it and dispose of it. Mark was upstairs in the bedroom, grounded for shoplifting King Don's at King's Korner; piecing together a puzzle that he could not have cared less about. Louise, meanwhile, was delegated to cleaning the kitchen.

Momma watched her for a long time before speaking. When she did speak, it was in a condescending manner, her voice dripping with a sweetness that was buried in bitterness and trickery. "You know what, Louise?"

"What?" Louise responded, much like a normal child.

"I remember when I was a little girl like you, my parents used to take a lot of vacations, like we do on Thursday nights. They used to leave us at home with a babysitter. Boy, we used to have all sorts of fun."

"Yeah?"

"Oh yes. I remember my big brother," of which Momma never had one.

That was how Mark knew that trouble was brewing. "He used to take care of us. Boy, oh boy, did we have a good time. We used to get wild and crazy, and my parents never knew about it. You know what? When my parents did find out, they weren't even mad. I bet you kids have fun when we're away square dancing, don't you?"

"Well..?" Louise responded, hesitantly.

"Oh, don't worry, Louise. If you kids do have fun, it's okay," Momma said very sweetly. Mark knew that Momma was warming Louise up. Whenever someone was nice to her, she came out of her shell. Momma tugged on another string. "Look at these. Do you want one of Daddy's donuts?" she offered.

"Oh, yes," Louise said, taking the bait.

"Here you go." Momma watched her eat it. "I bet that after we leave the house, Danny let's all of you out, doesn't he?"

"Well, yes," she answered.

Right about then, Mark was upstairs, feeling like he was going to be sick to his stomach.

"Well, that's okay. You kids should be allowed out. I bet you have a lot of fun, don't you? I mean, you probably watch television and go outside and play, huh?"

"Yes, Momma, we do," Louise answered. "But we're careful."

"Uh huh. I bet you have food out of the cabinets, too."

"Oh, no. We never do that," Louise defended. "We play and things. Sometimes, we just talk. Other times, we even play hide and seek except that Mark and Danny never let me win," she said, opening up. It was obvious that she enjoyed this rare, personal talk with Momma.

"Does Danny tell you that he's disobeying us?"

"No."

"What does he tell you?" Momma asked. Was her voice sounding somewhat strained?

"He tells us that we should never tell you what we do when you're gone."

"Now, why don't you go to your room and play?"

"But I'm not finished with my chores in here."

"Yes, Louise, you are finished," Momma said, an edge in her voice.

"Don't worry, Danny will take care of it. I have one more question."

"Yes?"

"Did you kids ever play 'doctor' while we were away?"

Louise hesitated. "Once we did."

As Louise went upstairs, Mark felt a panic well up inside the deepest reaches of his gut. He never had a chance to warn Danny. As he told Danny many months later, he had no idea that Momma would react quite the way she did. If he had, he would have jumped out the window to warn Danny of his impending doom.

"Danny, can I talk to you?" Momma asked Danny from the doorway to the garage.

He was still digging through his box of toys when Momma appeared, causing him to jump involuntarily. At first, he thought that Momma had busted him with his hidden toys.

"Yes, Momma," Danny answered obediently. He walked over to where she was standing. Judging from the look on her face, he had a feeling that he was in trouble for something. He knew that he had to watch his guard and he knew that something was wrong. The butterflies danced in his stomach while he tried to maintain a mask of composure. It was as if she could look right through into your soul sometimes and this was one of those times. He could feel it and it was immediately apparent that it wasn't about his toy box.

"I was just curious. How is the babysitting going for you?"

"What do you mean, Momma?"

"Does everything go alright? You don't have any problems keeping your brother and sister in line?"

"No. They're good," Danny said. He was not sure at that point where she was heading, but he wasn't pleased with where she was steering. He did his best to keep his eyes focused on her eyes. She could tell you were lying the moment that you looked down.

"So, Louise stays in the basement and Mark stays in his room, right?"

The way that she had asked the question made Danny even more suspicious. The thing was, he did not think that there was any way that his brother or sister would divulge their Thursday night secret. The only people who knew what was really happening was within their triangle. Even so, he had this strange feeling that he was walking into a trap, but what else could he say? "Yes, they stay in their rooms like they're supposed to."

"So, you have no problems and you conduct yourselves in the manner that you were told to?"

"Yes, Momma."

"And you think that you're doing a good job, obeying us?"

"Yes, Momma. We're all good when you're gone."

Momma crossed her arms across her chest. "Does that include playing 'doctor' with your sister?"

Suddenly, the smile fell away from Momma's face and Danny knew that he was in for it. When she raised her arm to belt him, he knew what was coming. He did only as was natural, raising his arm in defense, and Momma's forearm crashed into his.

If anything was a precursor to trouble, bad trouble, it was when a blow was shielded in defense. At that moment, Danny knew that things were going to get out of hand. It was the look of surprise in Momma's face and then the look of her own pain in realizing where the blow connected.

Mark and Danny had spent many a late night conversation talking about the 'beast' or the 'rage'. One could never guess when it would come out. They remembered times like the laundry room when it had flooded and Daddy's beast had come out. It was the difference between pain and sheer, irreversible terror. Daddy, when he was under an extreme amount of outside pressure, was the first to let this uncontrollable rage out. Momma's beast had only shown as far back as when they were being sued and Daddy had become distant. It was as if violence was the only way that she could keep the fragments of their family together. But, if a blow was shielded off, it was elevated to something higher, unsurpassed in intensity. Danny saw it coming in the redness of her face and the smallness of her eyes.

It was the same look that Louise must have seen when Momma lost her mind while beating her in the foyer. The only thing he felt was fear, clean and crisp in clarity. The type of fear where the bowels would let go without your even realizing what was happening. The worst part of it was that once the beast was released, there was nothing that anyone could do to stop it. It fought against all reason and rationality and the best that one could hope for, was to live through it.

Because, to a child under those raining blows death was a nearby and close companion.

Momma backhanded him across the face, her diamond ring slicing through his cheek as if he was a tender piece of veal. She lunged at him and threw him to the ground.

"You goddamned liar!" she screamed. She grabbed him by the hair and dragged him over to the cement threshold between the garage and the laundry room. He tried to stand, but he could not quite catch a grip. He could feel the edge of the threshold digging into the back of his head. The next thing that he knew, Momma was standing over him, her hands in a death lock on his ears and in his hair. She lifted his head up and slammed it into the threshold.

Again and again, she did it while Danny flailed uselessly. White sparks flared behind his eyes every time his head slammed into the cement. He fought the urge to throw up as the pain echoed in his mind. He started screaming as loud as he could, his head threatening to explode. Spittle sprayed on his face in her anger.

The beast was loose and God was nowhere in sight.

She yanked the dazed and bleeding boy to his feet and pulled him into the laundry room, slamming the door. His screaming would surely have gotten the neighbors' attention. But, with the door shut, his cries fell on deaf walls. Danny wet his pants, something he had not done in a long time. When Momma saw it, it was as if her rage was turned up one more notch. He had never been that scared in his life. Momma began smacking and hitting him until he was cornered by the walls.

"So, you like babysitting, huh?!" she said, cuffing him on the side of the head.

"Please...!" he tried to scream. His voice sounded muffled while his ears rang.

"You like disobeying?" she yelled, her foot slamming into his shin.

"Owww!!"

"You like to lie?!" she asked him at the top of her voice. Blow after blow rained down on him, until he fell to the floor. "You piece of shit for a son! We trusted you and this is what we get?" she screamed at the cowering figure in the comer. Momma began kicking him like a useless piece of meat, with no area protected, as hard as she could, in the shins, the ribs and even his face was not spared.

"Stand up!" she ordered him, grabbing him by the hair at the top of the head and yanking him to his feet. She clenched her fist, while yanking on his scalp, and rammed it into his face. In a reflex, his arm came up and hit her in the chest. Blood poured from his nose and splashed on the yellow-tiled floor. His head was reeling yet she would not stop. He screamed as loud as he could, praying that someone would intervene, praying that it would stop.

He felt himself slam into the wall. He dimly saw Momma's face pressed close to his own, sweat smearing her make-up, distorting her features. He could smell her breath and hear the rasping of air as it ran in and out of her lungs.

"We warned you, didn't we? You lying sack of shit! You have destroyed this family! You pathetic excuse for a human being! We warned you, didn't we?!" she screamed.

"Yes" Danny wailed.

For the moment, Danny lost track of time. The ringing grew to a continuous muffle while she slammed him into the wall repeatedly. He felt the blackening rushes threaten to overtake him. He would pass out at any second...

He was not sure when, but it stopped. All he felt was her yanking him out of the laundry room by the ear and upstairs to the main foyer. He could feel the wetness of the blood on his face.

"Get undressed!" she ordered him.

"Wh... w...what?" he asked, his breath coming out in short wheezes.

"You heard me, you despicable piece of shit! Get undressed!"

Danny stood there in disbelief. He thought that he was really going to get it then.

"I...I...I..."

"Don't you pull a Louise on me! You're dripping blood all over the floor!" she screamed. She grabbed his shirt and literally tore it off. She began to roughly wipe his face, smearing his features. "I am not going to have you run away again! Let's see how far you get when you're in the nude. Now, are you getting undressed or am I going to have to do it for you?!"

"No, I'll do it!" Danny screamed back, wanting to die rather than go through any more torture. He took all of his clothes off, hurriedly, and stood cowering in front of her.

Momma grabbed him by the ear and yanked him into the kitchen. She got a mop bucket out of the pantry and put it into the sink, turning the water on full blast until billows of steam rose from it. She threw a sponge in and set it on the floor.

"When your father gets home," she said, with a bloody fierceness in her eyes, "he's going to kill you! You think you got it from me? Huh? Well, it was nothing in comparison to what he's going to do you! While you're waiting for him, you can scrub every inch of this floor on your hands and knees. Do you understand me?!"

"Yes!"

"Listen, you naked ninny! While you're busy cleaning, you had better be saying some prayers because you haven't seen anything, yet!" Momma grabbed him from under the arms, digging her fingernails into his flesh. He screamed in agony as shockwaves of pain ran from his biceps to the tips of his fingers. "Now, get on your knees and clean!"

She threw him to the floor, grabbed him by the head and dragged him to the steaming bucket of water, yanking his arm and diving it in. Danny cried as the white hot heat stung and then numbed his hand. "I said, clean the floor! Now!"

Danny's numbed hand found the sponge, pulled it out. He started scrubbing as fast as he could. Momma kicked him the ribs one last time and stormed out of the kitchen, making her way upstairs.

"And don't you dare think about running away, you little creep," she screamed down from the balcony at the top of the stairs. "Remember, I have all your clothes and the only way that you'll do it is naked. If I catch you even thinking about it, I'll kill you before your father has a chance to lay a finger on you! Is that clear?!"

"It is!" Danny yelled up to her.

Danny fumbled with the sponge, his breath still surging in and out of his lungs, heaving. As he cleaned, he saw that he was wasting his time. For every wipe he made, blood dripped, making fresh marks on the floor and the water pink. His nose ran and his body ached.

There was only one thing on Danny's mind as he mindlessly wiped. He had to do it! He was more than thinking about running away, he knew that he had no other option. If what Momma had done to him was any indication of what was to come, he was not going to be around when his father came home.

Every limit had been crossed in human decency and there was no way that he could live through it again. He had to get out of that house quickly, naked or not!

He scrubbed and mumbled uncontrollably to himself. "Oh God, please help me! Please don't let it happen anymore. Please! Please...!"

After gaining some control, he crept to his feet and looked around the corner, up the stairs. He listened, fighting to keep his teeth from chattering.

He could not see his mother but knew that she must have been in the master bedroom. He could see the doorway to his room but it was shut. There was no way for him to get in there without Momma seeing him or hearing him.

Clothes! Where was he going to get some?

He heard the sound of the toilet flushing from Momma and Daddy's room.

It was then or never. The reverberating sound of the toilet would mask the sound of his naked feet running across the tiled floor of the foyer. He bolted, not worrying about his nakedness. He ran through the foyer and down the stairs toward the family room and, in no time flat, he was headed toward the laundry room, pausing at the adjacent bathroom. He dashed in and grabbed a towel, hurriedly wrapping it around his waist. He listened for the sound of his mother. He heard nothing, thankfully. He saw his blood-smeared face in the mirror. Quickly, he used the towel to wipe his face and then wrapped it around himself again. Knowing that there was no time to waste, he ran into the laundry room, pausing to open the door to the garage very slowly so as not to attract the attention of Momma. He pulled the door closed behind him and made his way to his bicycle. He grabbed it by the handlebars and ran it out of the garage as he clumsily hopped on and started pedaling.

Unfortunately, the damn thing was in tenth gear and it was a struggle to get it moving. He yanked the shift levers down, panicking when he saw the chain threatening to slip off of the gears. Suddenly, they caught themselves as he gained speed heading down the driveway. As the bike picked up speed, he almost spilled himself on the street by taking the turn at the bottom of the driveway a little too fast. The bike skidded crazily as he regained control, trying to think of where he was headed.

The only thing that was on his mind was getting out from under that roof as fast as he could. Then, the towel almost blew off. He grabbed it in time as he tried to maneuver the bike, picking up speed with every passing second, his mind, a jumbled panic of thoughts.

Robbie! The thought of his best friend flashed through his mind in an instant. He was there through the failed tape recordings and he would be there for this, Danny thought. He pushed his legs as hard as he could as he blew through "Doctor's Row" and down toward Brule road, where Robbie lived. He kept looking behind him, expecting to see Momma chasing him in the car. Danny bucked the wind and pushed himself even harder until his legs began feeling like lead.

Before he knew it, he was at the bottom of Brule road, with Robbie's house in sight. He hit Robbie's driveway a little too fast, skidding wildly and then losing control. The bike crashed into the bordering bushes while Danny flew over the handlebars. He didn't even feel anything. As soon as he hit the ground, he was jumping up just as quickly as the accident happened, the pain being nothing in comparison to what he had been through. Quickly, he wiped his face and then ran up to the front door, pulling the towel tightly around his waist. He pounded on the door, a little too emphatically.

"Yes?" Robbie's mother hollered from somewhere in the house. Danny looked toward the cement steps, attempting to regain some semblance of control. He was not running away, he...he had been swimming. That's it!

"It's Danny. Is Robbie around?" he asked, trying to keep his rushed breath at bay. It was difficult, especially knowing that Momma might be coming around the comer at any second.

"Sure, Danny," she answered cheerfully, upon opening the door. He saw a funny look cross her face. He looked toward the ground, shielding his face.

"Oh, I've been swimming and I wanted to tell Robbie about it."

"That's nice," she said, sounding as if she bought the story. "Do you want to come in?"

"No, thank you," Danny said, fighting the urge to check for Momma behind him.

"Suit yourself. Let me get him for you."

Danny stood there, for what felt like an eternity. Every sound made him think that it was the roar of Momma's car. Where the hell was Robbie?

"Hi, Danny," Robbie said, startling him with his appearance.

"It happened," Danny said in a panic, through the screen door.

"What did?"

"I've got to hide, Robbie!" He reached in and pulled Robbie outside as fast as he could. He just about yanked Robbie off of his feet as he pulled him around to the side of the garage, out of the sight of the street and any neighbors who might have been watching.

Robbie's face had a hundred questions written all over it. "What happened to you?"

"My parents! My mom! She lost it. Then, she said that my father's going to kill me!" he said quickly. It was as if he couldn't get the words out fast enough. "I ran away! You've got to help me! I don't have any clothes!" To prove it, Danny pulled the towel away and quickly put it back around him.

A look of disbelief was on Robbie's face. "Did you tape it?"

"How was I supposed to tape it? It happened so quickly that I didn't even have a chance to think about it!"

"Jesus, Danny!"

"You've got to help me, Robbie!"

"I don't know what to do!"

"Just hide me! Please!"

"Okay! Okay!" Robbie answered.

And so, the adventure began.

CHAPTER 14

THE GREAT ESCAPE

"The first thing that we have to do is get some clothes for you. Hold on a second, I'll be right back," Robbie said.

"What about your Mom?"

"What about her?"

"Don't let her catch you," Danny warned.

"Aw, Danny, don't worry about it. I've got normal parents, remember?" Robbie said. "But, just in case, I'll be careful, anyway." He gave Danny a quick supportive smile and went back into the house.

Danny sat down by the wall on the side of the garage, his towel still wrapped around him. He felt oddly vulnerable and his hands were still trembling uncontrollably. There was only one thing that he was still sure of at the moment: he was glad that he had run away and he was resolved in the decision that he was never going back. At that point, he wouldn't have cared if someone had told him that he was going to be living in a dumpster for the rest of his life. The only thing that nagged at him was that he did not exactly feel free. He felt like a dog that was on the loose who knew that his captors would be back to get him. As he looked into the shadows of the trees, he couldn't shake the image of his mother screaming, "When your father gets home, he's going to kill you!"

It seemed like forever and a day before Robbie returned. Danny had been daydreaming of various scenarios regarding his feared imminent capture when his best friend suddenly appeared, startling the hell out of him. He jumped.

"God, you scared me? And what took you so long?" Danny asked.

"Sorry about that," Robbie answered affably. "Here, put these on. I snuck them out of the house without my mom seeing me."

Robbie handed Danny a faded pair of jeans, an orange tee-shirt (which didn't amuse Danny with its billboard effect), some old white socks and a pair of dilapidated tennis shoes. Danny would not win any fashion contests but the clothes sure felt great after he had put them on. It took the feeling of vulnerability away.

"You look kind of funny," Robbie said.

"I do? Why?"

"Those clothes are way too big for you, for one thing. What's funny is that I haven't worn them for years because they're way too small for me."

"Hey, I'll invite you over for dinner at my house for a few weeks and I bet you'll fit in them in no time," Danny said sarcastically.

"The food that your parents serve is that good? No thanks," Robbie said.

"You're missing something, though."

"What?" Danny asked. "I know what it is. I need those shoes like John Travolta wears in Saturday Night Fever."

Robbie took his Detroit Tiger's baseball cap and dropped it on Danny's head. "There, perfect."

"I can't take this," Danny said. "It's your favorite hat!"

"Not anymore. It's your favorite hat, now."

"Look, Robbie," Danny said, a serious tone to his voice, "thanks for the clothes and stuff."

"Aw, no sweat. You may not be able to wear them to your senior prom, but they'll work. That's what friends are for, you know? Besides, my mom will throw a fit if she sees you running around naked. I get into enough trouble as it is," Robbie said with a smack on Danny's back.   "Hey, let's go out back in the woods so we can talk. I don't want your parents seeing you here. Now that would be trouble!"

The two boys trekked to the woods behind the house, to the fort that Robbie and Danny had built years earlier. It was made from excess lumber from a new house that had been built.   It didn't look new anymore, though, with its rain streaked walls and warped curves. Danny and Robbie could not have counted the number of secrets that they had shared there over years past.

The thing was, those past secrets were pretty minor compared to the ones that they were sharing now.

Once inside, they settled on the dirt floor. To anyone else, the fort might have looked ratty and run down but to Danny, it was a great haven from the terrors of the outside world. Robbie pulled out a couple of pieces of Watermelon Jolly Rancher Candy that had gone soft and gooey from being in his pocket all day.

"Here," he offered Danny.

"No thanks," Danny said out of habit.

"Would you just take it?" Robbie pressed him. Remember? You're not with your parents anymore."

"Sorry," Danny said. He proceeded to delicately work the cellophane off and then popped it in his mouth. Robbie followed suit.

"So, tell me what happened?"

Danny began the story with how the day had begun without any sign of danger. He proceeded to tell Robbie about the babysitting questions and then, finally, about Momma's explosion of anger and how it was nothing in comparison to what his father was going to do. He left out the parts where he had cried, giving Robbie the impression that he had done his best to take it like a man but it had gone too far. The rest was history. That was how he found himself at his best friend's house.

"Geez, Danny, that really sucks," Robbie said, snapping a twig in half.

"Robbie, I don't know what to do. The worst part about this whole thing is that I feel like a coward for running away."

"Why should you feel like a coward? You didn't have a choice. You were scared."

"Yeah, but my brother and sister are still there and I hate to think about what's going to happen to them. My mom wasn't kidding when she said that my dad was going to kill me. He's going to kill them instead! I know it!" Danny said vehemently. He embarrassed himself in front of Robbie by breaking out in tears. It felt like he was always crying. For once, he wanted to take things like a man and quit acting like a baby.

Robbie sat there, without interfering. He munched on his Jolly Rancher thoughtfully. "They're bastards, man."

"Yeah," Danny agreed.

"We shouldn't have bothered taping them. We should have just killed them, like setting the house on fire when you guys were supposed to be at school," Robbie said with a manly determination. "Man, can you imagine what would have happened if they had ever caught you or me taping them? We would have been dead meat for sure!"

"I told you that it was risky, didn't I? You didn't believe me. You kept telling me to get closer and closer and now you know why I was scared," Danny said.

"Okay! Okay! I screwed up, alright? I didn't know that they were quite that bad. Give me a break! Most parents..."

Danny cut him off. "Yeah, well my parents aren't most parents. The question is: What am I going to do now?"

"I'm not sure," Robbie said flatly.

The two boys sat in silence with Danny picking at his shoelaces and Robbie tracing trails in the dirt with his finger.

More than anything, Danny wanted to disappear, and pretend that all of this was someone else's dream. He felt tired and worn out with nowhere left to turn and no one left to help him. Part of him was tempted to lie down and go to sleep so that he could pretend that his life wasn't happening. But, he knew that he had to be an adult about the situation, especially considering that he didn't have a choice. He was in a state of flux while trying to think of what to do but nothing came to mind, deepening his resentment for what his parents had started.

"The worst part of it is," Danny said, "that I don't even have any proof that anything happened."

"Yeah, you do," Robbie retorted quickly.

"What kind of proof? I never had a chance to tape it."

"Your face!"

"Huh?"

"Danny, do you know what your face looks like?" Robbie asked.

Suddenly, Danny had a brief image of all the blood. There was the cut on his cheek from Momma's diamond ring. Then, the bloodied nose, not to mention all the spots on his body where he had been kicked and bruised. "Yeah! That's it!" Danny said ecstatic at the thought. "Come outside where it's light and take a look at me!"

The two of them crawled out of the fort and found an area where the sun went through the trees, unobstructed. Danny took off his newly acquired shirt, while Robbie proceeded to look at his back, much like a fellow baboon might preen another.

"Jesus, Danny!"

"What is it?"

"You've got red marks all over your back! You got the shit kicked out of you!" Robbie said, not hiding his surprise.

"Is it that bad?"

"Big time! Those marks may be red right now, but I can tell you from experience that they're going to turn into some mean looking bruises. I bet they get all purple and blue and they'll look even worse than they do now! Let's look at the rest of you."

Danny stood there as Robbie slowly walked around him, quietly inventorying the damage. He looked under Danny's arms and found the bloodied cuts where Momma's fingernails had gouged him. He looked at Danny's legs and saw where he had been kicked repeatedly, swelled in spots and the skin torn and bloodied in other spots. With Danny's permission, he felt around the crown of his friend's skull.

"Owww!" Danny protested vehemently.

"What'd I do?"

"Be careful! My head hurts!"

"Hold still," Robbie ordered him. His hand gently moved along Danny's head. "Yeah, you got a really good beating this time. Wow! If my mom ever did this to me..."

Every once in a while, Danny would jump involuntarily as Robbie's hand went over a particularly gentle spot.

"Your head is full of bumps. It's got little red dots all over it, too. Is that from where she pulled your hair?"

"I guess so," Danny said. "Owww! That hurts!"

"Sorry."

"Just be careful!"

"Man, Danny. We should do something about this. I hate to say it, but it's gotta be soon."

"Why's that?" Danny asked.

"Because this is the evidence that we've been looking for. If we're going do something, we can't wait until it heals up. Somebody has to see this!"

Robbie said. "Let's go back to the fort and figure something out."

The two made their way back and crawled in. They sat in silence, contemplating their plight. They both knew that they had an opportunity to do something and they had to do it right and they had to do it quickly. They knew that in a matter of days, the evidence would quickly disappear in the healing process.

One by one, Robbie placed ideas on the table and, just as quickly, Danny would shoot them down. First, Robbie said that he could show his own parents. Surely, they'd understand. Danny argued that it was too risky. How could they be sure that Robbie's parents wouldn't just call Danny's parents?

That would put them right back at square one. Robbie then suggested that they go to the police. Danny reminded Robbie of the phone call to the police, the night that Louise went to the hospital. The police wouldn't listen while it was happening, so why would they listen after it happened?

"Maybe I should just leave and go to another town," Danny said, the futility of his situation settling in.

"No, you can't do that. What about Mark and Louise?"

"I know, but I can't think of anything else to do."

"We have to think of somebody who'll listen," Robbie pursued, not ready to give up the fight that easily.

"I don't know of anyone."

"Danny, there's got to be someone we can tell. Don't you have any adult friends who'll listen?"

"No."

"What about one of our teachers?" Robbie asked.

Firmly, Danny said, "I don't trust teachers."

"Okay. How about a grandmother or grandfather?"

"I have a grandma, but I doubt that she'd believe me. Besides, she lives too far away, in Detroit."

"Hmmm," Robbie said, contemplating.

"See what I mean?"

"How about babysitters?" Robbie offered. "Don't you guys stay with one when your parents go on vacation?"

"They barely ever go on vacation."

"Oh. Well, how about..?"

Danny interrupted, "Wait a second!"

"What?"

"A babysitter! There is one that my parents always choose. Two years ago, when my parents went to Europe, we stayed with this really nice lady named Mrs. Thill. I don't know if she would work or not, but I just got to thinking that she likes us. She might listen, I'll bet on it!"

The boys discussed the pros and cons of telling her. Danny had known her before the problems had gotten as severe as they did. What he did remember, clearly, was that she had liked the kids. He remembered wishing that he had parents who were like Mr. and Mrs. Thill instead of who he had gotten stuck with. Danny was starting to think that she might be his best shot at resolving his predicament.

"No guts, no glory," Robbie stated.

"I've heard that before."

It was resolved. They were both going to make the trip across town to Mrs. Thill's house. Robbie left Danny in the fort while he ran home to ask permission from his mom if he could go out and play for a while. A short time later, he returned, knowing that his mother wouldn't go out looking for him. They both left, on foot, to Mrs. Thill's.

It took the better part of the afternoon to get within a few blocks of where she lived, since they had to minimize their risk by using all side streets to get there. Suddenly, Danny suffered a case of cold feet.

"I can't do it," he said firmly.

"You have to, Danny."

"I don't have to do anything," Danny said adamantly.

"Fine, Danny," Robbie said, not hiding his irritation. "Why don't you go back home so that your parents can continue beating the shit out of you over and over again, until you're dead? If you don't want to grow up and be a man about it, then there's nothing else that I can do," Robbie said, heatedly.

"I'm scared, that's all."

"I know. I'm as scared as you are. I don't even know why you're still alive. If I were in your shoes, I don't know what I would have done. All I know is that I'm lucky to have gotten the parents that I did," Robbie said. He took Danny by the shoulders. "The only way that we're going to have a chance for you to live with me is for us to do something about it. We've got to take the first step and we have to be strong about it."

"I know, Robbie. But, kids don't have rights. Only adults do."

"Listen to me," Robbie continued. "What has happened to you is wrong. I'm sure it is. A family isn't supposed to be like your family. All kids screw up once in a while. That's the point of being a kid. But, you're not supposed to end up in the hospital for it. The right people have to know about this! You're in control and you're strong. You're stuck with the job of helping your brother and sister, too. If you don't do something, what's going to happen to them? You told me that yourself! You need to find the right people through Mrs. Thill."

"I'll never find the right people," Danny said pessimistically.

"Maybe not, Danny. But we have to try."

"I know."

Robbie reached into his pocket and dug for his house key. He pulled it out and took it off the ring, handing Danny a white rabbit's foot.

"Here," he said. "This always bought me good luck. I think that you need it more than I do."

Danny took it and rubbed the soft fur beneath his fingers. "Thanks, Robbie. First the hat and now this?"

"You've been the best friend that a kid could ask for, you know? You'll always have me as a friend," he said, looking toward the ground. Danny thought that he looked like he was going to cry.

"You'll always have me as a friend, too," Danny said.

The two boys gave each other a hug, something that Danny had rarely done with anyone. Robbie shook his friend's hand and wished him the best of luck. He turned around and began his walk home.

Danny watched his figure grow smaller and smaller in the distance, all the while, rubbing the rabbit's foot between his fingers. When Robbie was out of sight, Danny felt a loneliness that seemed to rip into the deepest part of his heart. He had no choices left. He had to see Mrs. Thill, alone.

Butterflies, once again churned in his stomach as he walked the final block to her house. His palms were sweating as he made his way up her cement steps. He rang the doorbell, pausing momentarily, making sure that he knew what he was doing. His head and his back ached and throbbed. He could either be walking into a new life of freedom or he could be headed straight back to the unwelcome arms of his parents. If the latter was the case, those arms would kill him next time.

As he waited for someone to answer the door, he rubbed the rabbit's foot furiously.

He was scared. It was now or never.

CHAPTER 15

SEARCH FOR EVIDENCE

"Danny?"

"Hi, Mrs. Thill."

"What in the world are you doing here?"

"I just thought that I'd come by and say, 'Hi'."

"Well, come on in."

Mrs. Thill was just as Danny had remembered her. She was a large woman with light brown hair, which she usually left curled in a bun over her head. Whoever said that fat people were jolly, was right in Danny's eyes. Mrs. Thill was the epitome of that and more, being a loving and tender person. It was exactly why Danny had chosen her as his last resort. During the times that the kids had stayed there, Mrs. Thill was never seen without a smile on her face, being the exact opposite of who Momma was. She also served the best food that Danny had ever tasted, next to Grandma's, of course. No wonder that Danny wished that she had been his real mother.

"Would you care for something to eat?" Mrs. Thill asked, the first thing that she always asked the kids when they were there for a stay, as if food was as standard as saying, hello.

"Sure," Danny said, happy with the stall for time. As much as he wanted to be comfortable with her, he found it difficult to quell the butterflies in his stomach. There was so much he had to say, but he didn't know how or when to start.

Moments later, Danny had a plate of homemade chocolate chip cookies in front of him, complemented with an ice cold pitcher of lemonade.

"I thought that this might do the trick," Mrs. Thill said with a smile. "It's so damn hot out there that the heat is enough to drive a crazy man crazier."

"Thank you, Mrs. Thill," Danny said as he hungrily bit into a cookie. It felt like he hadn't eaten in years. The last thing that he had had was a bowl of puffed wheat for breakfast, which was akin to eating air, and his stomach seemed to remember that.

After Danny had voraciously munched down about eight cookies with Mrs. Thill watching him, she finally asked what brought him to her house.

"Ah, nothing. I just wanted to visit."

"Danny. I know children, and they don't walk all the way across town just to visit. Or, did you take the bus?"

"I walked," Danny said.

"So, what's wrong?" Mrs. Thill asked perceptively.

"Nothing. Really," Danny answered. He had lost his nerve in telling her and he did not know why. What did he have to be afraid of? His mind answered back just as quickly as the question had arisen. Remember Father Regan? She would love his mother's house and birds, just like he had.

"Is something wrong at home?"

"Well, um, not really."

"Danny? Tell me."

"I don't know what to tell you."

"I can see that there's something on your mind. Don't be afraid."

"I am afraid," Danny admitted.

"Why don't you start wherever you want and I'll sit here and listen? Now, what is it?"

"I ran away."

"Oh, no," Mrs. Thill said, leaning forward. A look of concern and worry settled on her face. "Why?"

"Well..."

And then he talked. He spit everything out, beginning with the belt and proceeding through his previous adventures with running away and why he had run away. He told, with increasing intensity, of how everything had escalated into something that he couldn't hope to control, anymore. He told of Mark's running away, and of Louise's visit to the hospital. He even told her of his empty promise to Mark and how he didn't think that he could have kept such a promise.

Mrs. Thill was obviously shaken at his tale. "And what made you run away today?"

"Because my mother lost her temper with me, the worst that I've ever seen. Well, next to what happened to my sister. Then," Danny said, trying to catch up with his breath, "after she was done with me, she said that Daddy was going to kill me when he got home! I'm scared because I know that she was serious. I had to run away," Danny said emphatically. "Mrs. Thill? We have to do something!"

"It's okay, Danny," she said. "Sometimes parents will get a little upset with their children. When we warn you to be afraid of your father coming home, it's only a figure of speech. It doesn't mean that it's really going to happen. Raising kids is a lot more difficult than it looks. You have to be more understanding," Mrs. Thill said, much to Danny's consternation and frustration. Evidently, she saw it on his face. "Look, Danny, I can talk to them and we can work this out. I've met your parents and I'm sure that they don't mean to hurt you. Lord knows, I've dealt with enough children to understand that much. Why don't we..."

Danny tried to interrupt her. "But, Mrs. Thill..."

"But, nothing, Danny. Look, I think that the best thing that we can do for you is to call your parents. You can talk to them over the telephone."

"Wait, Mrs. Thill..."

"Danny, this is for your own good. Don't worry," she said. "I know what I'm doing. They're probably worried sick over you right at this moment. What's your telephone number?"

"No, Mrs. Thill," Danny defiantly said. "I won't give it to you."

"Danny, please don't make this any more difficult than it already is," Mrs. Thill countered. It became obvious to her that

Danny was not willing to cooperate with her. She picked up the Marquette telephone book and rifled quickly to the "W's".

Danny watched her, growing angrier by the second. He could not believe that she was doing the same thing to him as the others had done. Had he miscalculated? Was she like all the rest of them?

Feeling cornered and frightened, the first thing that was on his mind was that he needed to escape. It was time for him to leave.

Mrs. Thill picked up the rotary telephone and started dialing.

Suddenly, Danny jumped up in protest. "No, Mrs. Thill!" he yelled. Without his realizing it, he jumped up and yanked the phone out of her hands. "You haven't listened to a word that I've said. Louise just went to the hospital! My parents are mad and there's something wrong with them. Nobody else's parents are like mine! Now, you want to send me back to them?! No way, Mrs. Thill. I thought that you cared about me. I thought that you cared about kids!"

"I do, Danny."

"No, you don't! You're like everyone else!" Danny yelled with intensity that he didn't know he had inside of him. In a role reversal, he mimicked what he had seen his father do to him so many times, "Oh, Danny reads too many books. Oh, Danny has such a wild imagination! Well, tell me, Mrs. Thill, did I get these from books?!" Danny screamed.

Much to the shock and surprise of Mrs. Thill, Danny suddenly began tearing his clothing off, article by article, until he was standing in front of her in his underwear. He turned around so that she could see his back.

"Did I get this from a creative imagination?!"

He was trembling from head to foot in anger and determination. He knew that he had been taught to treat adults with respect. He had never so much as even raised his voice to an adult, at least not the way he had to a stunned Mrs. Thill. He felt slightly remorseful for yelling at her, a lady whom he truly cared about, but his anger had overtaken all of his senses. The adrenaline rushed through his body, marking a trail of frustration. He stood there and tried to calm down but his legs were shaking so badly that he could do nothing but remain silent.

Evidently, it worked because Mrs. Thill was walking around him, her hand cupped over her mouth. "Oh, my," he heard her say, faintly, as if her breath was gone.

As she looked him over, gingerly touching the fresh wounds, she asked him to explain the origin of each, as best as he could.

Carefully, Danny reiterated everything that had happened on that nightmarish morning.

"I'm so sorry for not listening to you," she said tenderly.

"I'm scared of them, Mrs. Thill. Nobody has ever believed me. The best that anyone can do is to keep sending me back. I'd rather kill myself than go back to them!" he said vehemently. "It's usually okay for a while and then everything starts all over again. You've got to help me! I don't know what to do, anymore!"

Mrs. Thill embraced him into her full chest as he let his tears flow. She held him tightly as he fell apart, although he was partly grateful that it appeared that he had an impact on her.

After he had calmed down significantly, her hands running through his hair, she told him to put his clothes back on. "I've got to make a phone call in to work."

"Why?" he asked suspiciously, wondering if he was about to be tricked.

"I have to call my boss at work. Do you know what the Department of Social Services is?"

"No," Danny said, thinking that it sounded like a fancy name for the police department.

"We handle special cases like you. You aren't the only child to have suffered the things that you have," she explained carefully. "What has happened to you is very serious. You've convinced me that we have to do something. We want to help children like you."

"Are you going to send me back to my parents?"

"I don't think so, Danny. If we can prove that your parents have, in fact, abused you, which appears to be the case, then there's a good chance that we can get you into a foster home. Is that what you want?"

"Anything, Mrs. Thill," Danny said gratefully, relief in his voice. "Remember that my brother and sister are going through it, too. If I go anywhere, they have to go with me. If they stay there, they'll get killed by them! None of us should have to go back there. Ever."

"Leave it up to me, Danny," Mrs. Thill said. "Let's see what we can do."

She picked up the phone and called her work from memory.

"Hi, Charles," she said when she got the proper person on the line. "I've got a problem here. I've got a young man here by the name of Danny Wilcox, whom I've babysat for in the past. Ah, he's in a bit of trouble."

Danny looked on, praying that he was doing the right thing.

"No, no. He hasn't done anything wrong. He's run away from home and I believe that he's had reason to."

She squeezed Danny's shoulder in support.

"Yes, Charles, I'm serious. He's got marks all over him, the type that couldn't have been self-inflicted. I think that you had better take a serious look at him."

Danny wiped his hands on his pants.

"Yes, Charles. I'm quite aware of who he is. I also know that it's not going to be easy to file a six-fourteen against Dr. Wilcox but it has to be done and there's no other alternative. When you see him..."

Mrs. Thill stood up, as if she was emphasizing her point. "Charles, listen to me! I don't care if he's the son of the President of the United States! What has happened to this boy is wrong. This kid has been brutally beaten," she said emphatically in defense of Danny. She was pacing with the phone coil dangling behind her, an exasperated look on her face.

"No, Charles. We would not be liable. You must give me the benefit of the doubt and see him. Rest assured, that once you do, you'll understand."

Mrs. Thill listened for a moment and appeared to calm down as a deal was struck.

"Thank you, Charles. Danny thanks you ahead of time. We'll be down tomorrow afternoon."

She hung up the phone and looked at Danny, her hands on her hips.

"What's wrong?" Danny asked.

"Nothing, Danny. It just took a lot more work than I thought it would to convince him to, at least, take a look at you. It seems that your father extracted his wisdom teeth a number of years back. Can you beat that?"

"Everybody knows my father, Mrs. Thill. That's half my problem. Everyone thinks he's perfect."

"I gathered that," Mrs. Thill said supportively. "Anyway, here's what's going to happen. Tomorrow, you're coming down to my office. There are some people there who are going to look you over. As far as tonight is concerned, Charles is going to contact your parents and let them know that you're okay."

"Oh, no!" Danny exclaimed, a frightened look on his face.

"Whoa! Don't worry. He's not going to tell them where you are, if that's what you're worried about. I convinced him that you'd be in danger if you were returned home. At least I was able to get through to him that far. Legally, we have to tell them that much. We'll worry about the next step tomorrow, okay champ?"

"Please don't call me champ," Danny said. "My dad calls me that when he's upset at me."

"I'm sorry, Danny. Do you trust me, yet?"

"I think so, Mrs. Thill."

The rest of the night went without incident. Mrs. Thill made a feast for kings by cooking up a load of spaghetti covered with as much Italian Sausage as he could eat. He watched 'The Three Stooges. on television afterwards, curiously wondering why he was amused at their beat-em-up antics when he didn't find it anywhere near amusing at home. When he crawled into bed, he felt as if he had a new lease on life but wondered when it would end.

His dreams were filled with his parents. What if they caught him? What were they thinking now that he had gone so far? There was many a time that he found himself tossing and turning, vivid dreams capturing his imagination with colors of hitting, smacking and hair pulling, a fate that his brother and sister were forced to reckon with. When he woke in the morning, he felt more exhausted than anything, especially with the anticipation of what he was going to face that day.

It was Danny's turn to speak now.

The day broke as overcast and dreary with a threat of rain as Danny and Mrs. Thill made their way to the Department of Social Services. It turned out a more harrowing day than Danny could have imagined with one counselor after another interrogating him relentlessly. Pictures were taken of each and every bruise. As they pursued their investigation, a tape player recorded Danny's explanations. He wondered, for a time, if they weren't trying to catch him in a lie. Danny's stories remained consistent, although he had repeated the stories so many times that he felt like he couldn't even think anymore.

"So, why are you doing this?" a nameless counselor asked, his jowls bouncing with the question.

"Because I don't ever want to go home again," Danny answered firmly.

"Well, don't you think that you and your parents could work things out?"

"No, we tried that," Danny answered. "The only thing that ever came out of this was more beatings. I was the one who had to see the counselor, not them. Now, ever since my sister went to the hospital, I'm afraid that things are going to get worse."

"What hospital did she have to go to?" the counselor asked, his pen dutifully transcribing every word into a notebook.

"Ah, the hospital on Spruce Street, near the high school."

"And what night was that?"

"About six weeks ago, on a Friday night, I think..."

The interrogation and barrage of questions continued throughout the day, for three days in a row. Danny tirelessly answered each question, fulfilling his ultimate role as the protector, all in the hope that he would never have to live at home again.

After the third day of questioning, Mrs. Thill squeezed his shoulder supportively. "Well, Danny, it seems that the department believes you."

"Really?"

"Yes, really. Our counselors have been working overtime on this.

They've talked to Father Regan, they talked to the doctor that worked on Louise and they've talked to your neighbors. We finally got some corroboration to your story."

"What's that mean?"

"It means that other people have stepped forward to back up your statements."

"You mean that I have proof?"

"It looks like it, Danny. People were pretty shocked with your allegations. Everyone seems to know your father and it was pretty hard for them to believe that you weren't lying. See, people expect child abuse to happen only in high-risk families, where alcohol and drugs are abused, and in families that are broken and poor. What you've shown is that it can happen anywhere, regardless of social stature. You should be proud of yourself."

"Yeah?" Danny said, greatly encouraged.

"It took a lot of courage to stand up for your brother and sister. It takes an adult to do that."

"So, what happens now?" Danny asked.

"Somehow, we have to get through to Louise and Mark. It appears that they won't talk to us."

"I don't understand why not," Danny said. He figured that they would gladly step forward, if Momma and Daddy weren't sitting there.

"Well, the problem is that your father has gotten himself a lawyer. He's claiming that you made this up. We're trying to work around the law but it's turning out to be pretty difficult to speak to them."

"You'll be able to do something about that, won't you?" Danny asked, feeling insecure about the situation.

"I think so, Danny. You have a lot of people on your side."

"So, are we coming back here for more questions tomorrow?"

"No, we aren't," Mrs. Thill answered.

"Then, what are we going to do?"

"We're going to court. You're going to be able to tell a judge and a jury exactly what you've told us. Do you think you can do that?"

"Yes," Danny responded, determination in his voice. "I know I can."

It was the moment of truth, finally.

CHAPTER 16

THE TRIAL

"Are you sure that you want to do this?" Mrs. Thill asked, as they were preparing to leave for the courthouse.

"Yes, I'm sure."

"You're being quite a man about everything."

"Thanks, Mrs. Thill," Danny said. "It doesn't mean that I'm not scared, though."

"Remember, there's nothing for you to be afraid of. We're all here to protect you. Do you remember what to do?"

"Sort of."

"Let me tell you again," she said, placing a steaming plate of scrambled eggs and grits in front of him, heavy on the melted butter over the grits. "Now, eat this. You'll need the energy for today."

Danny dove in hungrily, smiling at the thought that nobody had to force Mrs. Thill's food down his throat. It was too good and probably explained why she was so ample in weight.

Mrs. Thill continued, pecking at her own plate, distracted by what they were going to face that day, "We're going to court to bring charges up against your parents. Those charges are going to state that you have been subjected to abusive behavior and that, in essence, the goal is to have you and your brother and your sister removed from that household. Do you understand that much?"

"Yes, Mrs. Thill. We've been through this a hundred times."

"If we have to, Danny, we'll do it a hundred more times. This is very important. Now," Mrs. Thill continued, determined that Danny was going to do everything right, "I'm sure that they're going to put you up on the witness stand. There will be a lawyer on your side and there will be a lawyer on your parent's side. Each, in turn, will be asking you questions. Answer them as honestly as you can, and be as accurate as you can on any details."

Danny looked at her and smiled nervously. "Boy, do I have details."

"Don't be afraid to tell every one of those details. This time, there isn't going to be a jury there. We have to prove that these charges have merit. So, your attention should be focused on the judge. If he believes you, then formal charges will be brought against your parents."

Danny finished a long drink of apple juice. He wiped his lips, saying, "I've got it so far."

"It's not going to be easy. You'll get a lot of pressure from the lawyers, both yours' and your parents'. I'm warning you ahead of time, your parents' lawyer is going to try as hard as he can to prove that you're lying."

"I'm not lying," Danny said defensively.

"I know that, and you know that. Your job is to make sure that the judge knows. Don't be afraid if a lawyer tries to intimidate you, he's just doing his job. Most importantly, don't be scared of your parents. They can't touch you in a courtroom. When you tell your story, stick to your guns. The moment that you think that you're starting to feel insecure, just look over at me," Mrs. Thill enunciated. "I'll be right there, giving you support. Just be strong."

"Believe it or not, Mrs. Thill, I will."

"Somehow, I know you will, too," she said softly.

"I have a question, though."

"What's that?"

"Will my parents try and come after me?"

"The only way that they can do that is through their lawyer. Don't think about it," she said. Mrs. Thill paused to straighten the buttons on her red dress. She had worn red so that, no matter where she was sitting in the courtroom, Danny would be able to pick her out easily. She took a deep breath and held Danny by the shoulders. "Let me be very honest about something, so that you're not surprised in the courtroom. Your parents are claiming that they have never harmed you at all, even on the day that you ran away to me. They said that you only got slapped on the back once, because..."

"That's a lie!" Danny said, infuriated.

"See? You mustn't do that in court," she pointed out. "Now let me finish. They said that you accidentally got a slap on the back because you hit your sister."

"Where do they think that I got all the bruises from?"

"They're claiming that you must have done it to yourself," Mrs. Thill explained.

Danny looked down, his appetite shot.

"Danny, you and I know that that would have been impossible to do. We also know that you're telling the truth. As long as you tell the truth, nothing will go wrong. Remember, we have pictures of what they've done to you."

"I remember," Danny said.

"We have tapes of your testimony, although their lawyers are arguing that they can't be submitted. We also have the hospital reports from Louise. Don't worry about a thing! There's so much evidence against them that there's no feasible way that they can lie their way out of it!"

"I'm worried," Danny said. "Things have never worked out the way that I've wanted them to."

"Well, this time, they will work out. Be strong on the witness stand and stick to the truth."

"I will."

"Are we ready to go to court?"

"Yes, we're ready."

Mrs. Thill straightened Danny's tie, a conservative striped tie complementing a navy blue suit that she had purchased for him at J.C. Penney's. Shortly thereafter, they were in her car, headed toward the courthouse. Danny kept to himself for virtually the whole trip, still feeling exhausted yet apprehensive at what he was about to face. His world had been filled with imagining every possible scenario as far as what was going to happen. He figured that it was best if he didn't look at his parents. If he did, he knew he'd break down and they would surely come after him. He'd resort to suicide before he ever went back to them.

One slap? *That* pissed him off. How could they say that? All of his life, he'd been taught to obey the Ten Commandments. Now, maybe he wasn't the best at following the Ten Commandments, but what about them?

They didn't obey the Ten Commandments so well. On the other hand, there was no commandment that said "Thou Shalt Not Hit Your Kids" even though there was a commandment that said "Honor Thy Mother and Thy Father".

What else was he supposed to do? Maybe God would understand and be on Danny's side for a change.

The courthouse was located a block from St. Peter's Cathedral, a lot smaller in comparison to the church. Its red brick facade loomed ahead, its walls about to hear the tale of Danny's harrowing experiences. For a moment, while Mrs. Thill parked the car, Danny thought that the building, with its dusty red stone exterior, looked almost ancient and forbidding to him. Mrs. Thill must have sensed his apprehension because she stopped to give him a firm hug before they walked up the steps to his fate.

As they walked through the brass embossed glass doors, Danny felt miniscule and unimportant. All around him, people hustled around in preparation for the day's proceedings. He saw a sign directing them toward a room straight ahead, its sign glaring in black and white: 'The State of Michigan vs Wilcox'. Danny's stomach rumbled with a zillion butterflies. He dropped his eyes to the orange marble floor as they walked in, not wanting to make eye contact with his parents.

With a squeeze of his shoulder, Mrs. Thill whispered to him, "Remember to be strong, Danny. There's nothing to be afraid of."

"I will," he whispered back.

Out of the corner of his eye, he accidentally saw the rest of his family. He couldn't take his eyes away from them, wondering what his brother and sister must have been thinking. They were standing quietly in a group on the other side of the courtroom, their faces showing no sign of emotion. Louise and Mark were dressed appropriately, in new clothes, as if they were going to attend midnight mass on Christmas. Daddy stood behind them, dressed in a dark brown suit while Momma stood by his side, wearing a black skirt with a light blue blouse.

Daddy's eyes made contact with Danny's. His jaw, ever so imperceptibly, jutted forward, not enough so anyone else would know, but enough to let Danny know, he wasn't pleased. Those eyes said, 'If I ever get my hands on you...'

Danny squeezed Mrs. Thill's hand. She returned her support.

Daddy and Momma said something to the man who was standing next to them, in the blue pin-striped suit. Danny surmised that man to be the lawyer that Mrs. Thill had spoken of. The man nodded his head toward Daddy, as if extending his permission for something. To Danny's discomfort,

Momma and Daddy strolled over to where he and Mrs. Thill were standing.

He felt like he was going to wet his pants as a ripple of fear ran through him.

"Thank you, Mrs. Thill, for watching our son," Daddy said, sarcasm ringing in his voice. "We really should have guessed that it was you behind these antics. How is he doing?"

"Fine," Mrs. Thill answered, her voice as cold as a stiff winter chill.

"Have you fallen for Danny's wild imagination, too?" Momma asked. "Or, should I say his lies?"

Daddy appeared to have nudged Momma into silence with a whisk of his hand.

"Maybe you know, that's for the court to decide," Mrs. Thill answered.

"Hmmm, we'll see," Daddy said.

For a moment, silence hung in the air until Daddy focused his attention on Danny. "How are you, son?" Daddy asked.

In the lousy fourteen years that Danny had lived at home, his father had never referred to him as "son".

"Fine," Danny answered, trying to be strong yet, at the same time, afraid for his life.

"Why are you doing this?"

"I have to," Danny responded firmly, his eyes averting Daddy's.

"Danny, Danny, Danny," his father said, shaking his head. "We're your parents and we love you. There's no reason for you to continue this charade, now is there? It's all over now. We want you to come home and we can straighten this out."

Obstinately, Danny answered, "There's nothing to straighten out."

"Look, if we've done something to hurt your feelings, we're sorry," Daddy said, extending his hand. "Let's call it quits, champ. Are we still friends?"

Danny looked at his father's hand and looked toward the ground.

"I'm offering my hand," his father said firmly.

Danny continued to ignore him, the tension growing with each passing second, not daring to give him the satisfaction.

Momma broke the silence, watching Mrs. Thill. "Poor Danny. He has a lot of problems, Mrs. Thill. It's sad to see that you were taken in by his stories, too. We're really very nice people once you get to know us. You should know better than anyone, that kids tend to exaggerate even the most simplest of things. We haven't done anything that any normal parent wouldn't do. Why don't we just brush this under the carpet and we can all resume being friends, huh?"

Danny felt Mrs. Thill's hand tighten on his shoulder. She was as mad as he was.

"As I've already said, Mrs. Wilcox, that's for the court to decide."

"If that's how you want to play," Daddy commented tightly, "then so be it. Oh, and Danny?" he added, "we'll talk to you later!"

Danny responded by blocking his father's voice out. His parents turned on their heels without another word and returned to the company of Mark, Louise and the man in the blue pinstriped suit. He looked at his brother and sister and, for the look that he got in return; he may as well have never been a part of the family.

"Are you okay?" Mrs. Thill asked.

"I'm more scared than before," Danny said softly. He couldn't get a grasp of what was going on. People seemed to be milling about, with no particular reason. He fought the urge to run off to the bathroom.

A man in a tan uniform walked up. He had a badge on his shirt and a very intimidating gun in his holster, giving him the appearance of being a policeman. "Are you Danny Wilcox?" he asked, a formal tone to his voice and demeanor.

"That's me," Danny answered, apprehensively looking at Mrs. Thill.

"The judge would like to see you in his chambers. Come along with me," he said.

Danny didn't remove his eyes from Mrs. Thill, as if to ask what was going on.

"I'm the guardian of the boy," Mrs. Thill said, intending to accompany him.

"I'm sorry, ma'am. The judge would like to see the boy alone. He'll be out in a short time," the bailiff said. "Come along with me, son," he said toward Danny.

"It's okay, Danny. I'm sure that everything will be alright. I'm right here, if you need me. Now, do as the man tells you," Mrs. Thill said with a squeeze of his hand.

Even though Mrs. Thill had said those words of encouragement, he didn't like what was going on. He felt what he thought a lamb must feel when he's headed toward the slaughterhouse. Her smile was weak and her eyes were as uncomprehending as Danny's.

Nervously, Danny followed the man through the double doors at the front of the courtroom, not daring to look toward his parents who were off toward the right. They entered a small, windowless room where the walls were lined with more books than Danny had ever seen, except for the Peter White Public Library. A man, dressed in black robes, was sitting studiously behind a large and ornate walnut desk, the cushion of a mahogany leather chair rising up behind him.

The first thing that Danny noticed about the judge was that he was surprisingly young given that he thought that all judges were old and gray haired, if they had any hair at all, that is. This man was as young as Father Regan.

"Have a seat," the judge said, motioning him toward a chair seated in front of his desk. "Do you know why you're here?" he asked, with a shuffle and a stacking of his paperwork.

"Um, to go to court," Danny answered in a tiny voice, noting the judge's nameplate as reading, 'The Honorable Judge P. Ferguson'.

"Why?"

"Well, I'm not sure," Danny said nervously. "I guess it's because I don't want to live with my parents, anymore."

The judge leaned forward on his desk. "And why don't you want to live with them?"

Danny knew that this was an important answer for him. He used his words carefully and deliberately. "Because I'm scared of them. They're always hitting us and I'm afraid that it's only going to get worse."

The judge took a deep breath and pondered Danny's response. He removed his glasses and started cleaning them with the cloth of his robes. He held them up to the light, checking their cleanliness. Satisfied, he put them back on and leaned forward on his elbows. "Do you realize what the implications are in regards to what you're saying?"

"Yes," Danny answered.

"Danny, let me explain something to you. These charges that you claim to have happened, well, they are serious. Your father has an impeccable reputation in this town. He's a very well respected man. Are you aware of that?"

"I know that," Danny answered, not particularly liking the direction where their conversation seemed to be headed.

"I'm not sure that you do, in fact, understand, son."

Danny sat there, picking at the cloth of his arm rest. He was doing his best to remain firm and strong, the way that Mrs. Thill had trained him. As long as he told the truth...

The judge restacked some papers and sighed deeply. "Do you know what perjury is?" he asked, a careful tone to his voice.

"No, sir."

"Well, when you walk into a courtroom, you're required to take an oath. You agree to tell the whole truth and nothing but the truth in front of the court and in front of God. Perjury is when you lie."

"I understand," Danny said, feeling as if he may as well have been standing on the moon.

"Do you know that I can put a person in jail for committing perjury?"

"Yes, sir."

"You don't want to go to jail, do you?"

"I don't understand, sir. Why would I go to jail?"

The judge adjusted his glasses on the bridge of his nose. He took a deep breath and let it out slowly, never removing his eyes from Danny's eyes. "For breaking the law."

To Danny, it felt as if a gavel had just made its impact upon his head.

"Now, son," the judge said slowly, "if I were to allow you to walk into my courtroom to continue saying the things that you have been saying, you would be committing perjury. I can't allow that to happen."

"You mean...are you saying that I'm lying?"

"The real question, it seems to me, is, why are you lying?"

"I'm not lying!" Danny said adamantly.

"Danny, I'm giving you a chance to come clean. As a representative of the law, I can't watch you destroy your father. You're a young man with your whole life in front of you and I'd hate to see anything get in the way of that. But, if you continue with this kind of talk, I'll be forced to do what the law mandates me to do. So, how about telling the truth?"

As the judge waited, Danny sat there, shock and disbelief across his face. This wasn't how Mrs. Thill told him it would happen! He was supposed to be on a witness stand and the judge was supposed to hear his story. He was supposed to hear what happened, how it happened and why it happened.

Danny exploded, knowing that it was his last chance to do anything. "Judge Ferguson, you've got to listen to me! I'm not lying! I never did lie! Everything that I told Social Services was the truth. I swear it was!"

"Consider yourself lucky that I do not charge you with sexual misconduct, as well. Your parents told me what you did," the judge said. He directed his attention toward the man who was standing behind Danny. "Bailiff?"

The officer stepped forward and motioned for Danny to stand up. Danny turned around as his hands were put behind his back. He could hear the sound of metal and chain clinking as he felt the cold steel of a pair of handcuffs, tightening around his wrists. He was stunned.

"Son, this is a serious matter here," Judge Ferguson said sternly. "You've left me no other choice but to sentence you to two years at the St. Mary's Rehabilitation Center Boy's Home in Houghton. Your actions, of late, are not befitting to your living with your parents. This is for your own good. After some time there, I hope that you'll understand the ramifications of your actions. Unfortunately, I think that this is best for all parties concerned."

"But...?" Danny tried to say.

"Bailiff, you had better take him," Judge Ferguson said, closing the matter once and for all.

The man pulled Danny out of the judge's chambers. All the while, a million thoughts ran through Danny's head. The first was disbelief while the second was the fast realization that he had just been railroaded. Sadly, Danny never found out exactly what happened on that fateful day. It could have been that his father had thrown some money around. Or, it could have had to do with the man in the blue pinstriped suit, more than likely a lawyer, who pulled a nice tricky maneuver. Or, it could have been that Danny's story was so incredible, against a man of such a worthy reputation, that nobody would believe it. The fact was: Danny felt like he had been made a mockery of, and he was back to square one, meant to suffer the consequences.

As soon as the bailiff got Danny back into the courtroom, Danny surprised the officer by breaking free of his grasp.

"I never lied!" he screamed as ran pell-mell across the courtroom. The officer unsuccessfully tried to grab him. Everything in the courtroom dropped to a hushed silence as everyone's eyes turned toward this fourteen year-old boy who looked as if he was losing his mind.

"Come on!" he yelled to no one in particular. "Somebody has to believe me! Please!"

Suddenly, he was in front of his parents, still handcuffed. "How could you do this to me?"

Momma looked down, as if embarrassed by the sight. She shook her head and managed an uncomfortable smile as if to say, where did this deranged boy come from?

"Mark!" Danny said to his brother. "Tell them that I was telling the truth!"

Mark's eyes looked at Momma and Daddy and dropped to the floor.

"Louise! Tell them about the hospital! Tell them about the foyer! You could have died!" Danny screamed.

Although her eyes were red, flooded with tears, she, too, looked away.

Suddenly, the officer grabbed Danny. Danny was no match for him, subdued into a horrifying silence.

"I'm sorry about that, Dr. Wilcox," the bailiff said, pulling Danny away.

"Such a shame," Daddy responded, shaking his head.

The bailiff walked the boy down the main aisle of the courtroom, a hundred eyes watching but no one saying a word. A movement toward the doors, revealed Mrs. Thill, fighting her way down the aisle.

"Danny! Danny! What happened? "

"Ma'am, please step back. We're taking the boy into custody," the officer commanded.

"Mrs. Thill!" Danny interjected to the protest of the bailiff, "They don't believe me! You told me that they'd believe me! They're taking me to jail!"

"You can't do that!" she said to the bailiff. She reached forward, to pull Danny toward her.

"Ma'am! Step back!" the officer demanded. "We'll have you arrested for obstruction of justice!" he said, yanking Danny away. He called toward the front of the courtroom. "I need some assistance over here, now!"

The next thing that Danny knew, he was being escorted out of the courtroom doors, his energy sapped and drained. The last sounds he heard as he left with the law were the shrill screams of Mrs. Thill.

"Danny! Danny!"

At the bottom of the courthouse steps, a police car waited, an officer standing behind the opened rear door. One of the officers grabbed the top of Danny's head so that it wouldn't hit the roof of the car, and pushed him inside. The door slammed shut as the waiting officer ran around the front of the car and hopped in, slamming the car into drive.

Danny looked out the back window only to see Mrs. Thill running down the steps, her red dress blowing in the wind. It would be the last time that he would ever see her.

The rest of the afternoon was spent in driving to the juvenile delinquency home in Houghton, about two and a half hours from Marquette. They drove up U.S. 41 into the deep reaches of the forest-covered Keweenaw Peninsula, with both the officer and Dan enjoying a stony silence.

Dan didn't think much of cops, anymore.

He stared out the window as his wrists ached uncomfortably. He was as angry as he had ever been. What went wrong? How could they not go to court, with all the pictures of his bruises? What happened to the hospital records? Did he have to die to save his brother and sister? While he was in jail, what was to become of Mark and Louise?

The car slowed when they reached County Road 33. In the distance, Dan could see a whitened steeple framed against a cloudless sky, above a gray weatherworn church, the only structure that could be seen for miles. The only exception was the bridge towers that connected Houghton to Hancock. The police car slowed and turned into the gravel driveway. The officer stepped out and opened the door, removing Dan's cuffs immediately.

"Well, you're home, Dan," the officer commented.

A fairly young, bearded priest casually walked to the car where they were standing. "Hello," he said affably. "You must be the visitor that I'm expecting. What's your name?"

"Dan Wilcox," he answered sullenly.

"Well, the pleasure's all mine. Why don't you come in and meet the rest of the boys? We're excited to have you as a part of the family. My name's Father Healy," he said, extending his hand.

Dan shook it weakly, not pleased about being the middle of nowhere with a bunch of strangers.

"The boys are in the living room. I want you to introduce yourself, okay?" the priest said.

"Sure," Dan responded coldly.

The officer waved and backed out of the driveway while Danny and the priest walked up the steps toward the rectory. He was led into the living room where he saw ten or fifteen boys waiting anxiously, some sitting on ragged furniture while others were parked on the floor. They all looked older to Dan, being sixteen or seventeen years-old...and they looked tough and street-worn.

Father Healy led Dan to the front of the room, under the close scrutiny of their watchful eyes.

"Now, tell your new roommates who you are," he instructed firmly.

"I'm Dan Wilcox."

"Tell us why you've been sentenced here. Don't worry, it's a ritual. Every one of your roommates has had to do the same thing upon their arrival."

Dan could feel their eyes watching him but he could not return their stare.

He was ashamed and embarrassed. "I don't know," he finally mumbled.

"Dan!" Father Healy commanded sternly. "Tell us why you are here!"

Dan bit his lower lip, determined not to start crying. He had no other alternative, again. These people didn't know him from Adam and they didn't care. It was a new world now with a new set of rules. The cards were dealt the way they were and he had no choice but to play them out, one by one.

He cleared his throat, holding his head as high as he could muster. "I'm here because I lied about my parents. I told everyone that they beat me and it was a lie. I committed perjury," he said. "It's nobody's fault but mine."

"Good, Dan," the priest said. "It's a start."

"May I go to my room?" Dan asked, his eyes dropping to the floor.

"Yes, you may. I'm sure that it's been a long day for you, hasn't it? It's down the hallway and it's the second door on the left."

"Thank you," Dan mumbled. He thought about saying, "You win again," but kept his mouth shut.

He stepped out of the living room and walked down the hallway, fighting the tears the whole way. The walls were colorless and grimy, flecks of paint peeling and worn. The bed was un-sheeted and stained.

He sat on the bed and then lay back as the filtered sun warmed his face. He turned on his side and stared at the wall, silent and determined.

He wasn't going to cry.

In the background, in a distant room, he could hear a tape playing, tinny and live, "I have never been so lonesome and a long way from home. Somebody help me...somebody help me..."

His tears made the mattress wet.

CHAPTER 17

THE STIRRING OF SKELETONS

Suddenly, it was nearly four decades later as I tried to come to terms with an answer on voir dire as to whether or not I had experienced domestic violence. The ballpoint of my pen rested on the questionnaire. The easy choice would have been to make no mention of it. It was unlikely that anyone would know the difference except for me.

I suspect that I am not the only potential juror to struggle with a particularly sensitive question such as domestic violence. I am not the only one to have experienced it and, even though each of our experiences is different, the results still manifest themselves deep within our souls.

The trick is to be honest. There is no reason to be wordy, just succinct. How could one explain a lifetime of hell in a few short words?

I took a deep breath, said the serenity prayer, and penned in my response, thinking that I had the wisdom to know the difference between what I could change and what I could not. I could not change my past. I simply wrote, "I took my parents to court for child abuse in 1976." Later in voir dire, when asked whether I had served time, I stated that I had served six months of a one year sentence for perjury when I was a juvenile.

It would take another three weeks before I would learn whether I had made the cut to be a juror. It was one of the most difficult periods of the trial. My mind was filled with regret in mentioning my history with domestic violence. I said a lot of prayers during that period and had convinced myself that it was unlikely I would be selected.

All potential jurors are admonished officially to avoid speaking about their trial to anyone. I could not share my feelings of self-doubt. I was prohibited from even speaking to a friend. I was trapped within my own thoughts for what felt to be an interminable amount of time. Even worse, the dreams and nightmares of my old family life surfaced as I slept. I woke each day feeling uncomfortable and out of sorts.

During that time, I thought of a trip Mark and I had taken in 1991 to attend his ten-year class reunion. Mark was in his late twenties while I was cresting thirty. I had not been in Marquette since my father had dropped me off at a Greyhound station in 1979, the day after I graduated from high school. His job as a parent was legally done; since I was close to eighteen and it was clear he did not want to see me again. Mark had left Marquette in the early eighties to be a pilot in the Air Force.

One of the first things we did when we got back to the town of our youth was to visit the courthouse where my trial had occurred. It should not have surprised either of us that there was no record of the proceedings. It did not help that the years had erased from my memory the name of the judge who had convicted me.

We made our way to Shiras Hills where our house was. We walked up the two hundred foot driveway and tried not to discuss the worst of some of our memories. We walked up the front steps and rang the doorbell. A doctor who had purchased the house ten years prior answered it. We explained that our father built the house, and we had lived there as children.

"How is your father?" he asked.

"He died a few years ago of cancer," my brother said.

"I'm so sorry."

"We left something here," Mark said. "It's hidden in the basement. Would it be okay if we retrieved it?"

The doctor graciously let us in. It was strange to see the house decorated with someone else's things.

I followed Mark to the basement. He grabbed a step stool and began lifting the panels in the ceiling. "I wish I had a flashlight," he said.

I handed him a lighter.

After a time, he began retrieving items. One by one he handed them down. It was a collection of Hot Wheels and model airplanes that he had hidden up there so that Daddy would not find them and throw them away. It was remarkable seeing fragments of the past.

We graciously thanked the homeowners and left, proud of those treasures from our childhood. Just as we reached the bottom of the driveway, I saw Dr. Pugh, the same neighbor that had lived across the street from our childhood.

He hardly recognized us since we had grown up but quickly warmed up.

"Did you ever hear any kids yelling or screaming from our house?" I asked.

"It was a long time ago," he said slowly.

"It was," Mark said. "Surely, you heard or saw something, didn't you?"

Dr. Pugh was clearly uncomfortable. He kicked at a pebble on the ground absentmindedly. "There were times that I heard kids being punished. Yes, I heard a lot of yelling."

"Did you ever see anything?" Mark asked.

The neighbor rubbed the back of his neck. "I remember your dad beating the crap out of you when you dropped all of your newspapers on the ground at the bottom of the driveway."

"Why didn't you do anything?" I asked.

"I thought about it," he responded reluctantly. "I wanted to call the police but then again, how people discipline their children is their own business. It's just not something I wanted to get in the middle of."

A short time later, we parted amicably. For Mark and I though, it was verification that the horrors in our mind were not figments of the imagination. The toys we had recovered were a reminder of how close Mark and I were and that we had each saved each other's life at one time or another although many years past.

"Do you remember the day you took Mom and Dad to court?"

"I've never forgotten it," I said.

"I don't know if I ever told you but just before we went to court, Dad made Louise and I clean all the blood from the back seat of Mom's car."

"What was the blood from?"

"Remember when Mom took us to the hospital after hitting Louise with a Spray N' Wash can? Apparently, since it was nighttime, no one noticed the blood until the day of court. Dad was pissed," Mark said.

"I bet his lawyers never saw it."

"Nobody did and nobody checked," Mark commented.

A week after completing the written voir dire, the potential jurors who remained were brought back to the courtroom for the verbal aspect of voir dire. I sat in the jury box with the other jurors and waited to be questioned on my written responses. I was most concerned about being asked questions about my parents and my history with domestic violence. My hands were sweaty all day as I anticipated my being called on by either the prosecutor or defense attorney. When the end of the day came and we were dismissed, I was shocked when I had not been called on all day.

Over the next week, I said a lot of prayers and tried to focus on the things in my life that I could control. Although I tried not to think of the past, it loomed in the back of my mind, a great weight of darkness and insecurity.

The day I was selected as a juror was a day I will never forget.

When the bailiff called my name, I felt a great sense of relief. Somehow, despite overwhelming odds against my being selected, less than a tenth of a percent chance, I had broken through a paper ceiling. I thanked God in my mind because I felt He had everything to do with my being there. I was surprised, honored and somewhat intimidated that I found myself in that position. I vowed that I would do the best I could do.

There are thousands of jurors every year who find they have to answer a difficult question in voir dire, one that stirs memories of trauma and unresolved issues. Most of those jurors, regardless of their responses, will never be selected. Many of those jurors, who truly want to be a juror, will wonder whether their frank and honest admissions were the reasons they were not selected. What each of those jurors does not know is that their greatest victory was being honest during the process, whether it is in the written or verbal voir dire process. By admitting the trauma, the potential juror had made the first step in growth from victim to survivor.

Over the next three months, I did what jurors are supposed to do. I arrived each day on time, I took notes throughout the proceedings and I questioned why I was selected against so many others who were probably more qualified than me. In those three months, I heard nothing about domestic violence and was able to tune that part of my past out. It was not relevant and, therefore, I was able to lock it away in my mind.

It was the death penalty phase that caused everything to change and for my past to rear its ugly head. The defense team witnesses presented our jury with mitigating factors to consider when making the final analysis.

One series of witnesses were psychologists who were meant to illuminate the effects of domestic violence on the defendant. It was not until the third phase did I realize I was selected because of my experience. Although I knew I was there to consider my past, I found myself defensive of it in my mind. How could a defendant who murdered in such a manner be given a pass just because there had been some abuse in her life?   I had not gone on to murder so how could I defend such a position from the defense team?

It was remarkably strange to hear the professionals speak of the effects of domestic violence and how it impacted victim's lives. I knew I was there to decide the fate of the defendant and felt guilty when I applied their testimony to what I had experienced.

I learned that domestic violence was about power and control. I learned that the behavior of the abuser affects the victim in a multitude of ways not the least of which was Post Traumatic Stress Disorder. I realized that the nightmares I had suffered for years were a manifestation of trauma from domestic violence.

I discovered that I drank not because I liked to drink but because I was self-medicating. I drank to keep the nightmares away. The testimony was meant for the defendant yet I learned that what I had experienced was not as abnormal as one would think.

Finally, it was the third phase of deliberations, the phase where we considered whether the defendant should live or die for her crimes. It was easily the most contentious and difficult piece of the trial. The three of us who had experienced domestic violence found ourselves telling our stories to the rest of the jury. It was our collective decision to decide whether the defendant had actually experienced domestic violence and whether it later influenced her behaviors later in life.

Those of us who shared our stories did not tell them to elicit empathy. We told our stories because it was the truth. It was not easy to tell our stories just as it was not easy to hear the stories of what human beings can do to each other. The law told us we must consider our experiences.

Our secrets had become important. Our secrets had value. Our experiences were for a greater purpose; ones we had not seen when we suffered the trauma. In the strangest of ways, the trial had offered therapy for questions unresolved in our minds.

It had been a simple question asked in voir dire and it bloomed like a flower months later. Had I chosen not to mention my experience with my parents in voir dire, I am confident I never would have been selected as a juror. Should I have chosen to ignore my past, I would have been dishonest.

Then, the day came when we finally made a decision.

CHAPTER 18

REDEMPTION OF A JUROR

Three months after the trial, I was three-quarters of the way through the writing of, 'Brain Damage: A Juror's Tale', the story of the trial I had just been a part of, when the phone rang. It was a private investigator.

"Do you know Louise, Mark and Dr. Wilcox?" he asked.

I wished I had not answered the phone. I was suspicious. "Why do you ask?"

"I was given a retainer by your mother many years ago. She is trying to reach out to you. You were a hard person to find," he said.

"Where is she now?" I asked, a bit taken aback.

"They moved from Michigan in 1980. She lives in another state. It appears your father passed in 1987."

He had not given me much information that I did not already know. When I learned my father was dying of cancer, I had written a letter home asking to see him before he died. The response letter from my mother said that I was no longer welcome home. I did not need to be told twice.

"What about Louise?" I asked.

"She is institutionalized near where your mother lives," he said.

I wondered whether the people who treated her were aware of the abuse she had suffered. I highly doubted it.

"I need a few days," I said.

He agreed to give three days. I spent those three days in a mental turmoil that featured a recurrence of nightmares and unsettled thoughts. I could not stop thinking about the crimes that were done against us as children. Had it not been for the trial, I do not think in retrospect, I thought of my parents' actions as criminal. Maybe it was not illegal to beat your kids senseless back in the seventies. It was a time that people kept their disciplinary actions behind closed doors. 911 Emergency calls and Child Protective Services had not existed. The many protections and safeguards that are in place now were not in place then.

I spent three days holding back tears until I made a decision, one that I put in the book I was writing. The victim was not obligated to go back to their abuser, no matter who the abuser was.

When the private investigator called back, I told him I preferred not to have a relationship with my mother. He appreciated my response and said he would keep our contact private. She would never know he had found me. I was good with that.

I went on to attend trials and to write books. I was fascinated with our justice system and how it worked. I think what drove me the most was my great empathy for victims of extreme tragedies. For every awful experience, there was some measure of good to be derived from it, no matter how distant and unreachable it seemed. Justice had a way of working out and it was in a large part due to jurors who did the right thing when asked.

I had been one of those jurors and I was honored to be part of it.

One would assume that once a jury has made a decision, been recorded in the trial docket, that each juror would be content. In my case, though, I often regretted some of the mitigating factors I used in deciding that the defendant should get life instead of death. Each time I doubted my verdict, I thought of the incredible amount of time we spent in deliberations. We had done what the law told us to do even though discomfort surfaced long after the trial was over.

Two years later, I received a call from the producer of Investigation Discovery's 'Deadly Sins', a cable true crime show with Darren Kavinoky. The show wanted my input on the trial of the defendant we had spent so many months discussing. I agreed to do the show but wanted my interview set the same day as the family of the murder victim. Although our decisions affected their lives, I had not had the opportunity to meet the survivors one on one.

A month or so later, we finally met. As much as I knew in my heart that we as a jury had committed every ounce of energy into doing the right thing, I still carried guilt that we had not given the defendant the ultimate penalty. It was hard to second guess the deliberation phase and the multitude of issues that arose between twelve common people selected to make the most difficult of choices.

The victim's survivor hugged me hard. I apologized for not voting for death.

"Don't you understand?" she asked. "We never wanted the death penalty. We did not want to go to court every time the killer made a motion to appeal. It would have gone on for years. We, as a family, prayed you would not make us go through that."

I had a surprised look on my face.

"You did as you were supposed to do. I thank you for your sacrifice. You did the right thing."

A moment of peace washed over me the like the warm rising tide of an ocean. There had been an end to this segment of my life's journey. One would like to have thought that things naturally worked out. I knew better, though.

God had a hand in everything including justice.

He presented a simple question in voir dire, which forced me to come to terms with the greatest horror in my life. I was no longer a victim. I was a survivor.

It all began with a simple prayer, one that I have now said two thousand nine-hundred and eighty days in a row, my eighth AA birthday.

"God, grant me the serenity to change the things I can, accept the things I cannot, and the wisdom to know the difference. I am grateful for the roof over my head and the opportunities God has given me. I am most grateful for allowing me to come to terms with my experience and hope you will offer strength to those experiencing domestic violence. I ask that you give those people around the victims the strength to say something if they see something. If this is what you want me to do in life, then I am content. If there is something more, I am ready. Continue to give me the courage to take it one day at a time and to do the next right thing.

Amen."

CHAPTER 19

EPILOGUE

Dear Dad,

I thank you for giving me a place to live and for food on the table. I appreciate your telling me the difference between right and wrong.

I wonder what life would have been like had you not used the belt as a teaching tool. Would it have made your life more difficult? Would we have made more mistakes as children? Would we have caused harm to someone if you had not used the belt to teach us?

I know that the day you left this earth you hated me. I can understand that. In your mind, I must have looked the enemy to you. I ruined your reputation. I embarrassed you in a court of law. Your best defense was that you disciplined with a heavy hand. You did it to make us better people.

What I have learned is that physical abuse is evidenced by any actions that leave a mark. The belt left many marks. I still have scars on my legs which remind me of your black wing-tipped shoes. I learned from you.

I never want to be like you. You could not control your anger and frustration. You created victims where there should have been none. You scarred each of us for the rest of our lives. You said you wanted the best out of us and the only way you could accomplish it was by being the worst to us.

I would rather have been raised poor and be loved than to be raised rich and then abused. I am now at the age you were when you were hitting us and I understand less why you thought it was appropriate. It was never appropriate. The wrath you laid upon us, as children, was criminal.

I take strength from taking you to court. I did the right thing. When I see behavior like yours, I say something.

Although the dark times will always be deep in my heart of memories, I will go forward carrying thoughts of what could have been. I will do my best to make this world a safer place to live in. I will do all I can to help those who have been through what I and my brother and sister went through.

I wish you peace for eternity.

I forgive you.

Danny

The end.

NATIONAL DOMESTIC VIOLENCE HOTLINE: 1-800-799-SAFE (7233)

NATIONAL CHILD ABUSE HOTLINE: 1-800-4-A-CHILD (1 800-422- 4453)

Secret Life of a Juror:

Voir Dire – The Domestic Violence Query – "A Juror's Perspective" Series: Book 4

Also Written By Paul Sanders

Brain Damage:

A Juror's Tale The Hammer Killing Trial (2015) – Book 1

Why Not Kill Her:

A Juror's Perspective The Jodi Arias Death Penalty Retrial (2016) – Book 2

Banquet of Consequences:

A Juror's Plight The Carnation Murders Trial of Michele Anderson (2017) – Book 3

Beyond the Pale:

Rogue Juror The Death Penalty Trial of Joseph McEnroe (Coming 2020) – Book 5

Follow Paul Sanders

Twitter: The 13th Juror MD

Facebook: Paul Sanders

Website: The13thjurormd.com

Dear Reader,

If my story moved you, I would be honored if you rated and/or left a review on Amazon. It helps reach more people like you. Thank you so much!

Paul Sanders

Made in the USA
Middletown, DE
19 June 2021